SENSITIVE ISSUES
IN THE WORKPLACE

SENSITIVE ISSUES IN THE WORKPLACE

A Practical Handbook

Sue Morris

The Industrial Society

First published in 1993 by
The Industrial Society
Robert Hyde House
48 Bryanston Square
London W1H 7LN
Telephone: 071–262 2401

ISBN 1 85835 023 9

British Library Cataloguing-in-Publication Data.
A catalogue record for this book is available from the
British Library

Typeset by: The Midlands Book Typesetting Company, Loughborough
Printed by: Lavenham Press
Cover design: Integra Communications, London

The Industrial Society is a Registered Charity No. 290003.

275290

CONTENTS

INTRODUCTION

The aim of this book is to provide basic guidelines to employers on how to deal with a range of sensitive issues in the workplace.

It is therefore important for organisations to establish a framework for dealing with such issues so that problems are tackled fairly and consistently based on carefully established principles rather than on an ad hoc basis.

Increasingly employers are recognising the need to care for their employees' well-being at work by tackling problems previously considered to be personal problems that should be left at home rather than brought to work.

For example although it has undoubtedly been going on for years, it has only recently been accepted that issues such as harassment and bullying contribute extensively to stress-related sickness absences. Organisations have only just begun to be concerned enough to tackle the problem rather than to brush the matter under the carpet.

For many years it was accepted practice to drink at work, particularly at business lunches or functions, as part of the normal way of getting to know clients better and to forge business relationships. Now it is generally accepted that work and alcohol do not mix.

Smoking has become a burning issue and many employers are introducing no-smoking policies — often with a great deal of resistance from a minority of smokers who may come from all levels in the organisation!

This book sets out the steps that should be followed when dealing with these issues to ensure that employees' problems are handled sensitively and fairly whilst remaining within the law.

VIOLENCE TOWARDS EMPLOYEES

There are a number of jobs where employees are at risk from being abused or assaulted by members of the public or their customers while carrying out their normal everyday duties or even when they are off duty.

Such abuse may be as a result of mental disorder, drunkenness, drug taking or simply because a person is potentially explosive or violent.

Jobs which are particularly at risk of abuse may include:

- Security officers

- Transport and delivery staff

- Care workers including nurses, doctors, social workers

- Those who care for the mentally ill

- Housing officers

- Prison officers

- Bank, building society and post office staff

- Department of Social Security and Department of Employment staff

- Traffic wardens, police, ticket inspectors

- Public house stewards

- Taxi drivers

- and many others

Employees who work alone and those who visit people in their homes are, perhaps inevitably because of their isolation, those most at risk of attack during the course of their daily work.

NATURE OF THE ABUSE

Abuse may be of a physical or verbal nature. For example physical abuse may include violence, often with the threat or actual use of weapons, which may result in a range of minor to major injuries or even death. Verbal abuse may include serious or persistent harassment or bullying which may include sexual or racial harassment.

THE EFFECTS OF ABUSIVE BEHAVIOUR TOWARDS EMPLOYEES ON THE EMPLOYER

Unless employers take positive steps towards minimising the risks to employees of being exposed to abusive behaviour, they will find it increasingly difficult to recruit and retain good staff. The cost of continually recruiting to replace leavers will more than outweigh the cost of providing training and support to those exposed to abusive behaviour.

Employers who lack concern and do not support employees who are at risk of abuse will become known. Such a firm will gain a reputation as an organisation to be avoided.

Those staff who remain may become demotivated and they may eventually end up suffering long periods of absence as a result of their own incapacity caused by their working conditions. This in itself may be costly to the employer, resulting in heavy sickness benefit liabilities as well as the cost of providing temporary cover.

THE EFFECTS OF ABUSIVE BEHAVIOUR ON THE INDIVIDUAL

Apart from the effects of violence from which employees may need time to recover physically, the mental stress and anxiety that can be caused by working in a threatening environment may take much longer to get over.

Personal confidence may be lost and an employee may have great difficulty in going back into the same environment through fear of the same thing happening again. Long periods of ill health may be experienced and the individual may feel incapable of pursuing his or her chosen career because of the continued exposure to abuse without any backup from the employer.

DUTIES OF THE EMPLOYER

As with other forms of behaviour which affect individuals eg bullying, sexual or racial harassment, the employer has a common law duty of care as well as a personal duty, under the Health and Safety at Work Act 1974, to take reasonable care for the health and safety of employees at work which includes:

- Providing a safe place of work and access to it

- Providing safe systems of work

- Providing adequate information, instruction, training and supervision to ensure safe working

All employers are required to take out Employers Liability Insurance against liability for "bodily injury or disease" sustained by their employees and arising out of and in the course of their employment.

The mere occurrence of an accident or dangerous incident does not automatically impose liability on the employer, but if he or she is found to be negligent he or she will have breached his or her duty of care. In other words, an employer will be found to be negligent if steps are not taken to eliminate a risk which he or she knows or should know is a real risk and not just a vague possibility.

Breaches of this duty of care may be pursued both through the civil courts under the tort of negligence or through Industrial Tribunals on the basis of constructive dismissal.

The standard of care and the adequacy of the preventative measures that must be taken must be balanced against the cost, practicality and effort involved in offsetting the risk. Employers may be able to show that they have exercised their duty of care in response to a claim of negligence by demonstrating that they have followed an accepted or common trade or industrial practice provided that it was not an inherently dangerous practice.

For example in Keys v Shoefayre Limited (1978), Mrs Keys was concerned about the security of her shop following an armed robbery. The District Manager's only suggestion to alleviate her fears was that she kept high denomination notes in a plastic bag in a drawer under the cash desk. The request to instal a telephone was rejected on the basis that it was not company policy. After a further robbery at the shop Mrs Keys left, and successfully claimed that she had been constructively dismissed.

The employer's personal duty of care is different from the employer's vicarious liability whereby he or she is responsible for the actions of others eg employees, contractors who may cause damage through their acts or omissions while acting on his or her behalf. It is therefore up to the employer to ensure that he or she

appoints competent people and that adequate information, instruction, training and supervision are provided to ensure safe working.

Employees have a statutory duty under the Health and Safety at Work Act to take reasonable care for their health and safety and that of others, to co-operate with their employer on health and safety matters and not to intentionally or recklessly interfere or misuse anything provided for health and safety purposes. A failure to do so may result in prosecution of the employee and such actions may be used in mitigation by the employer.

However, if it can be reasonably foreseen that deliberate acts of violence or skylarking may cause damage and an accident or damage occurs, then it may be viewed as a breach of the employer's duties if he or she has not provided a safe system of work, adequate supervision or reasonably competent employees, and in such a case the employer may be liable.

Under the EC Directive which has been introduced through the Management of Health and Safety at Work Regulations 1992, employers now have a duty to co-operate and co-ordinate with others where workplaces are shared or used by others who are not employees, eg self-employed persons or contractors.

This means that employers have a duty of care to ensure that safe systems of work have been devised, that adequate instruction is given and the necessary protective equipment provided even where employees work away from their employer's place of work under the control of another party.

TACKLING THE PROBLEM

Abusive behaviour towards employees is on the increase, and it is therefore essential to set up procedures and policies for dealing with such instances in working environments where they are likely to occur. The following guidelines may be helpful depending on the nature of the circumstances:

ESTABLISH WHAT ABUSIVE BEHAVIOUR IS

Employees and employers need to have an understanding of what constitutes abusive behaviour so that employees do not feel that they must just accept situations that occur as an inherent risk in the job about which nothing can be done.

They should be encouraged to raise any such difficulties without being made to feel guilty or that they are personally responsible in some way for what has occurred.

REPORTING OF INCIDENTS

Procedures should be established and published so that employees know how to report abusive behaviour and to whom.

This will enable the employer to investigate fully and take whatever steps are felt necessary to deal with the matter, eg by taking action to minimise the likelihood of a recurrence or where possible removing the source of the problem. It may be appropriate to provide the employee with further training in how to identify, prevent and, where necessary, diffuse such problems.

It will also demonstrate to employees that the organisation cares for their safety and wellbeing and that such problems will be taken seriously.

Employers in any event have a statutory duty to report all injuries and dangerous occurrences. Under the Reporting of Injuries, Diseases and Dangerous Occurrences Regulations 1985 (RIDDOR) employers must report to their enforcing authority (usually the Health and Safety Executive (HSE) or the local authority) any accidents or dangerous occurrences which result in employees being absent from work due to incapacity for more than three consecutive days.

All other injuries regardless of how minor they may appear must be recorded in an approved Accident Book.

ASSESSMENT OF RISK AND PREVENTATIVE ACTION

Under the EC Directive implemented through The Management of Health and Safety at Work Regulations 1992, employers are required to "adequately assess the risks to the health and safety of their employees" and "the assessments should be in writing including a record of any groups of employees especially at risk". "Employees must be provided with information on risks to health, protective and preventative measures, evaluation procedures, safety specialists and special risks."

This places a duty on the employer to look at the risk of abuse of each type of job, taking into account the nature and context of the interaction between employees and clients, customers and the general public. This will enable the employer to identify preventative measures that can be put in place to minimise the risk.

Preventative measures may vary widely depending upon the nature of the work. For example:

- Many banks and building societies have now installed security screens around the cash tills and photo-alarm systems to give their staff greater protection from potential robberies.

- If staff such as health visitors or social workers are required to work alone, for example visiting people in their homes, then joint visits may need to be considered where there is a potential risk of physical abuse occurring. A system of tagging files for potentially dangerous visits will alert staff of the need for extra caution to be taken where this is already known.

- Employees should be instructed to leave the address where they are going and the time they expect to return with a responsible person so that their organisation is alerted if they have not returned or made contact within a reasonable period of time.

- Mobile phones, phone cards or pocket alarms may be provided for employees who are out of contact with colleagues so that they have a means of calling or attracting help in emergencies.

In addition, under the Regulations, employees must be advised of the risks and given appropriate advice, information and training so that they understand and can act in such a way as to minimise the risks.

TRAINING OF STAFF

Training will be helpful in a number of different ways both in terms of prevention as well as cure!

As stated above, employers have a duty to provide adequate advice, information and training to minimise risks to the employee's health and safety. This includes making people aware of the potential risks as well as what they personally can do to minimise those risks.

As with all company policies and procedures, employees should be trained to ensure that they understand what the policies and procedures concerning Tackling Abuse are intended to achieve, and how they should be applied in the event that they need to use them.

Job training should not be confined to the "technical" skills needed to undertake the employee's job but should include specific skills needed to ensure his or her own safety. For example, interpersonal skills training will enable staff to deal effectively with clients, customers and the general public in differing situations.

Depending upon the nature of the job this may include an awareness of how to identify situations which could turn to verbal or physical abuse and how to diffuse such situations, as well as ensuring that the employee's own approach and manner is conducive to the type of work which he or she is undertaking.

AFTERCARE

Support and counselling may well be needed for employees who suffer from abuse during the course of their work, to enable them to regain their confidence and self esteem.

It is important that victims of abuse feel able to continue working or, if they have been off work due to their incapacity as a result of abuse, to be able to return to work and resume their duties in the knowledge that their employer is supportive of their feelings and anxieties.

PROFESSIONAL AND FINANCIAL ASSISTANCE

Depending upon the circumstances, the employer may feel that it is appropriate, with the employee/victim's permission, to take out criminal proceedings against the offender at the organisation's expense.

Alternatively, legal and/or financial support may be provided to the employee so that he or she personally can initiate proceedings against an offender.

A number of organisations now take out insurance to indemnify those employees who have to work with potentially violent clients.

BULLYING

WHAT IS MEANT BY BULLYING?

Bullying is the intentional intimidation or denigration of an individual through the misuse of power or position in the workplace.

Whilst bullying is most frequently associated with management bullying those at a lower status to themselves, it can and does frequently occur between employees of a similar status to one another.

Whereas racial or sexual harassment may be more obvious to identify, there may well be a fine dividing line between an aggressive style of management and bullying.

Examples of bullying behaviour include:

- Setting of unachievable objectives and timescales

- Insisting that the management way is the only correct way of doing things

- Frequently "changing the goal posts"

- Setting of "trick" problems

- Public "dressing downs" whether justified or not

- Continual nitpicking about minor issues

- Asking individuals loaded questions about themselves

- Continually making derogatory statements about an individual

- Calling individuals by offensive names

In the past it was thought that only those employees who were over-sensitive or touchy were likely to complain that they had been bullied in the workplace, and consequently their complaints were frequently ignored.

However, research has shown that the incidence of bullying at work is far more extensive than was originally thought, both in terms of the seriousness of incidents and also the number of occasions when they occurred.

THE EFFECTS OF BULLYING ON THE EMPLOYER

REDUCED EFFICIENCY

Employees who are being bullied will, unless they are extremely tough indeed, eventually suffer stress and anxiety from the behaviour towards them which will have a detrimental effect on their work performance.

They may find it increasingly difficult to take any initiative or make decisions for fear of criticism or retribution.

The amount of work which they are able to tackle will diminish as an increasing amount of time is spent worrying about their problem, and mistakes — often costly — could occur.

ACCIDENTS IN THE WORKPLACE

Not only will the standard of work performance be affected but there is also a danger that with their attention elsewhere employees may be unwittingly careless. Accidents could happen not just to themselves but even to others in the working environment.

POOR WORKING RELATIONSHIPS

Relationships within the working vicinity are bound to deteriorate, and this will eventually lead to poor morale and reduced motivation of other employees as well as the person affected by the bullying.

It could lead to industrial unrest.

INCREASED EMPLOYMENT COSTS

If individuals do decide to leave rather than put up with the situation then the cost to an employer will be high. For example, recruitment costs will include advertising, time spent interviewing, training and supervising a replacement employee.

THE EFFECTS OF BULLYING ON THE INDIVIDUAL

The effects of bullying on the individual can be far-reaching. For example:

FEAR OF RETRIBUTION

Unfortunately it is not uncommon for many employees to feel unable to raise their complaints for fear of retribution. They may believe that the person carrying out the bullying is invincible and that any action on their part to stop the behaviour will result in their being further victimised rather than resolving the problem. This fear may well be compounded if there is a major difference in status between the bully and the victim.

FEAR OF NOT BEING BELIEVED

It may be that the bully is in a fairly senior position with influence in high places. This will make it seem impossible to an employee under attack to accept that he or she could be believed in preference to the more senior person. He or she may well also feel that if the problem was made known, then other senior people might jump on the band wagon and behave in a similarly bullying manner.

Even if the victim is of a similar status to the bully it may be that the standing of the bully in the organisation appears more established, perhaps through length of service or through the personal relationships which he or she has established with colleagues at a more senior level. This may make the victim feel more vulnerable in the conviction that the bully is more likely to be believed.

Instead, individuals will continue to work under increasingly difficult conditions to the detriment of their work performance and as often as not to the detriment of their health.

LOSS OF SELF CONFIDENCE

Typically individuals may find that their self-confidence in their ability to do the job is slowly destroyed, as is their self esteem. They may even start to believe that the abuse and criticisms that are levelled at them are deserved! Often, a person in this situation may react by trying even harder to be nice, co-operative and willing only to find that he or she is bullied even more.

LEAVING EMPLOYMENT

The easy way out may be for employees to leave their employment to avoid continued contact with the bully.

However, it is very difficult for employees to find alternative employment in the current economic climate. Whereas before they might have chosen to find new jobs instead of putting up with bullying, they may now have no alternative but to say and put up with it rather than risk being unemployed.

EMOTIONAL DISTRESS AND ANXIETY

Emotional distress may affect the health of the individual, resulting in side effects such as anxiety, sleeplessness, depression and other stress related problems. Other outward signs may include the deterioration of personal relationships, hostility and irritability where this is out of character.

CASE STUDY

When Lee was promoted from a senior secretarial post to Assistant Manager of the Records Section, relationships within the Records Section slowly began to deteriorate.

Ben, the Senior Records Clerk who reported to Lee, had been employed by the company for some years and was generally well thought of. His appraisals had always been good and although it was recognised that he had reached the limit of his capabilities, he was well respected in his current role.

Initially Lee and Ben appeared to work well together but then the situation started to change.

Mistakes started to come to light which Lee openly blamed Ben for. Deadlines which Ben had

> **Case Study** (continued)
>
> always met were missed and his level of sickness started to increase. Lee started to complain that Ben was inefficient and could not handle even the simplest change in procedure. In fact it was Lee who was perpetually changing the instruction unnecessarily so that Ben was unable to keep up with the new requirement. Each time he failed he was derided and made to feel stupid.
>
> Eventually Ben resigned, unable to face tackling the problem with Lee. It was not until history repeated itself with another employee who worked for Lee that the bullying came to light.

TACKLING THE BULLY

One of the difficulties which employees face when trying to tackle a bully is being believed, particularly by their seniors. This is particularly so if the bully is being complained about to his or her "peer" group where there could be close working relationships and even social relationships. Inevitably the bully is more likely to be believed than the person making the complaint.

HOW THE EMPLOYEE SHOULD TACKLE THE PROBLEM

If an employee believes that he or she is being bullied and informal attempts to resolve the situation amicably with the bully have failed, then to be able to progress the matter further it is important that the victim keeps careful and detailed notes of conversations and when they occurred. Other correspondence or paperwork relating to the bullying should be kept so that they can be produced as backup.

For example, if recommendations have been made by the employee in a report which conflict with what the bully is telling everybody then the report can be produced to put the story straight. If the bully is publicly giving a false impression about an employee's absenteeism then a copy of the doctor's certificate will provide proof of the true state of affairs. Memos or letters from the bully which give an indication of his or her vindictiveness should be kept as evidence of his or her attitude to the employee.

Individuals should ask for colleagues who have witnessed the bully in action to provide written statements of what they have seen or heard so that they can be produced in evidence. If necessary, the statements could be submitted without identifying the colleague if there was a fear of retribution.

Once sufficient information has been gathered to support the employee's allegations then he or she should write to the bully setting out details of the matters which he or she has found of concern. The bully's response should be kept as part of the evidence. If there is no response, then that in itself is of significance and should be noted by the employee making the allegation.

By putting together a catalogue of evidence it will be much easier for the employee to convince management that his or her allegations have substance and that the matter is one that must be resolved.

As with other forms of harassment, employees who wish to raise a complaint in the workplace should be able to approach their Personnel Manager or another senior manager with their allegations. There should also be provision for them to seek assistance from their trade union or employee representative or another colleague of their choice. If counsellors have been appointed to help with problems of harassment then they should be able to help with problems of bullying.

HOW THE EMPLOYER SHOULD TACKLE THE PROBLEM

As with other forms of harassment, it is essential that the employer should take the complaint seriously.

There should be scope for the employee to raise the complaint either through the normal Grievance Procedure or, if one exists, through a special complaints procedure for dealing with allegations of harassment. The guidelines previously described for dealing with both sexual and racial harassment provide the basis of a model procedure.

ESTABLISHING WHETHER THERE IS A GENUINE PROBLEM

When a complaint is made, it is important to establish whether or not there is a problem of bullying or whether the employee making the complaint is simply being vindictive for his or her own reasons.

Even if a complaint has not been made, the organisation should be concerned for the psychological health of its employees as well as the physical aspects of health and safety. Even if a problem found is a minor one initially, it could escalate and get out of hand if the matter is not dealt with.

There are a number of ways in which an organisation can find out what is going on. For example:

- a change in the atmosphere

- a change in the attitude of employees

- increased absenteeism

- increased staff turnover

- reduced initiative and creativity

- less concern with quality and productivity

The circumstances surrounding the individual making the complaint should also be explored. For example:

- What has their track record been like in the past in terms of performance, attendance, attitude etc.?

- References from previous employers

- Have they recently transferred to a new area?

- Is there a new supervisor or manager over them?

- Has labour turnover or absenteeism increased amongst other employees recently in that area?

EMPLOYEE'S REDRESS

If an employee fails to resolve a complaint of bullying despite having raised the matter through the appropriate company procedures and subsequently resigns, then he or she may take his or her complaint to Industrial Tribunal on the basis of Constructive Dismissal. The grounds for the complaint would be that the unfair treatment to which he or she had been subjected was sufficient reason to justify his or her resignation.

LOOKING BEHIND THE PROBLEM

If it is acknowledged that there is in fact a problem it is important to try to understand what has caused the behaviour of the bully. Steps can then be taken to resolve the issue at the root of the problem, rather than just by taking disciplinary action.

Bullying tends to manifest itself as a result of conflicts within an individual or within an organisation.

CONFLICTS WITHIN INDIVIDUALS

For example, an employee may have been the subject of bullying at school, at home or even in his or her past work-places. Such treatment may have left him or her with a lack of confidence in his or her abilities or relationships with people so that when he or she is in a position of authority with power and influence over others, he or she may unwittingly be attempting to get his or her own back on society. It may be that a person who has suffered this type of stress in the past is unsuitable to be employed in a position where there are pressures on him or her that are likely to bring about this type of behaviour.

Bullies will select their victims for a variety of different reasons. It may be their popularity, ability or that they appear unable to stand up for themselves and are easy targets for bullying.

Occasionally a bully may pick on an individual who resembles someone who has hurt him or her in the past or someone he or she could not get on with such as his or her mother-in-law. Subconsciously bullies may treat their victims in the same way that they themselves were treated, without even realising what they are doing.

Personal problems in the home environment may affect how an individual behaves at work. This may include marital problems, financial problems etc. While some leniency may be understandable in tackling the problem, if it continues and it starts to impact on other employees then it should not be used as an excuse to push the problem under the carpet.

The bully may suffer from mood swings caused by drugs, alcohol or a medical condition which may need to be addressed.

It may be that in-depth counselling may help the bully to overcome the problem, or it may be possible for the individual to undertake personal training in developing interpersonal relationship skills or assertiveness training of a non-aggressive nature.

CONFLICTS WITHIN ORGANISATIONS

The style of management within an organisation may contribute to the conflicts and pressures that occur. For example in a highly competitive organisation where employees are dependent upon one another for their results or maybe even their pay, the pressure will be on for everyone in the team to be pulling their weight. If there is an individual who is perhaps not up to the standard of the others — or even perceived not to be up to standard — then it may be the norm to give destructive criticism and call that person names rather than to try and tackle the problem.

In some organisations difficulties and mistakes are not discussed and handled openly but instead become the subject of gossip and apportioning of blame, whether or not it is deserved.

HELPING THE EMPLOYEE TO RECOVER

In-depth counselling by either an outside counsellor or a trained in-house counsellor will help the employee to re-establish his or her self-confidence and personal esteem. It may be that training programmes to develop the employee's assertiveness and other social and interpersonal relationship skills will be of assistance. Training in managing stress is another area which may help in learning to cope with the situation.

SEXUAL HARRASSMENT

WHAT IS MEANT BY SEXUAL HARASSMENT?

Essentially, harassment is defined as behaviour which an individual finds offensive and unwanted. If the behaviour is welcome then it will be treated as friendly and wanted.

Although Sexual Harassment is not specifically defined under the Sex Discrimination Act 1975 (as amended) it does provide that harassment on the grounds of gender can amount to unlawful discrimination. This means that if a complaint of sexual harassment has not been properly investigated nor has action been taken, if appropriate, against the harasser then an Industrial Tribunal may infer that unlawful discrimination has occurred.

The EC Code of Practice on the dignity of men and women at work defines sexual harassment as "unwanted conduct of a sexual nature, or other conduct based on sex affecting the dignity of men and women at work". Examples of sexual harassment behaviour may include:

PHYSICAL BEHAVIOUR

Unnecessary physical contact such as touching, patting, pinching or brushing up against another person.

Seeking sexual favours for promises of promotion or other rewards.

Sexual assault.

VERBAL BEHAVIOUR

Sexual advances or propositions.

Continued suggestions for social activity outside of work after it has been made clear that such suggestions are not welcome.

Offensive flirtations, embarrassing remarks, innuendos or lewd comments.

NON VERBAL BEHAVIOUR

The display of pornographic or sexually suggestive pictures.

Leering or staring suggestively at another person's body.

Making sexually suggestive gestures.

THE EFFECTS OF SEXUAL HARASSMENT IN THE WORKPLACE

Apart from the moral aspects of creating a working environment which respects an individual's personal dignity, the "cost" to an organisation in practical terms of failing to do so can be considerable. For example:

HIGHER ABSENTEEISM

A harassed employee may find it easier not to come to work rather than have to face his or her harasser. In the longer run it could lead to anxiety or stress related illnesses which could have been avoided.

RESIGNATIONS FROM EXPERIENCED STAFF

Employees may decide to resign in the belief that they will not be believed or supported in their claims of harassment. This may result in well-trained, experienced staff having to be replaced and re-trained at significant cost to the employer.

REDUCED EFFICIENCY

Inevitably, if employees feel under anxiety or stress as a result of being harassed, then their effectiveness will fall while they are mentally trying to cope with these additional worries and pressures. Output of work is bound to drop, more mistakes are likely to be made and accidents could occur.

PERSONAL CONFLICTS IN THE WORKPLACE

Personal conflicts are likely to be both time-consuming and disruptive not just to those personally involved but also to those working around them. It may even lead to violence.

FINANCIAL COSTS

Time and money spent in defending claims together with the potential costs of compensation can be high in cases where the employer has failed to take action in a potential case of harassment.

At Industrial Tribunal the amount of compensation that may be awarded is up to a maximum amount set by the State and reviewed in April each year. The amount for the year 1993/94 is £11,000 including injury to feelings.

An employee may be able to claim for unfair dismissal where the potential maximum award may be as high as

- £6,150 basic award plus

- £11,000 compensatory award, including injury to feeling, plus

- £10,660 additional award for failing to re-engage or re-instate.

Breaches of an employer's common law duty of care for an employee's health, safety and welfare while at work and to provide a safe system of work may be pursued in the High Court and are not limited by any maximum amount.

WHO IS LIABLE IN CASES OF SEXUAL HARASSMENT?

The law allows for action to be taken against individual employees as well as the harasser's employer.

In addition to an employee's liability for his or her own actions, employers can also be held liable for the actions of their employees. Employers will always be liable if they are made aware of the harassment but fail to take any steps to remedy it.

CASE STUDY

In the case of Johnstone v Fenton Barns (Scotland) Ltd (IT Scotland 1989), Mrs Johnstone was employed in a turkey processing factory. She had first complained when a colleague hung a turkey neck from his private parts and he asked a young female employee "how would you like that?". In a second incident Mrs Johnstone claimed that the same colleague sung a song which included the words "Put your lips round my balls, Mrs Murphy". Although the man concerned denied using those words as they did not rhyme, he agreed that he had sung "Put your gums on my plums, Mrs Murphy". In two further incidents she heard her male colleagues discussing their sex lives and had made it clear to them that she found it offensive but they had laughed at her.

Even though Mrs Johnstone had not taken exception to all the dirty stories that she had heard, the Tribunal were satisfied that the four incidents referred to were offensive to her and that she had not been able to persuade her colleagues to stop.

The Tribunal concluded that, "If a man, working alongside a woman, converses or behaves lewdly with other people in the vicinity within earshot of the woman, and the woman has made it clear that she finds such conduct to be offensive, then any future similar occurrences must be regarded as having taken place against her wishes and thereby directed against her."

On that view all the incidents of lewd conduct, conversation and singing which occurred after she first complained and which she found offensive, must be regarded as treatment meted out to her which she, as a woman, was vulnerable to in a way that a man

Case Study (continued)
would not have been. It thus falls within the concept
of discrimination by means of sexual harassment. She
was awarded compensation of £3,731 which included an
amount for injured feelings.

It is not a defence to claim that an employee who harasses
another employee in the workplace is acting outside of the
sphere of his or her employment and it is therefore of no
consequence to the employer.

CASE STUDY

In the case of McPhee v Smith Anderson
& Co Ltd, (IT Scotland 1989), Miss McPhee was
employed as a machine operator. She claimed that her
chargehand was habitually calling her a prostitute and
had on several occasions put his hand up her skirt and
grabbed her bottom. The chargehand denied these
allegations but accepted that he was known at work as
the "phantom bumfeeler".

The employers argued on the basis that they were
not liable for the harassment as the chargehand was
acting outside the sphere of his employment. The
Tribunal held that as the acts were done in the course
of his employment, both the chargehand and the
employers were liable. Not only were the employers
liable for the acts of harassment but because they had
failed to respond to Ms McPhee complaints once they
had become known, they were also liable for causing
a "detriment". Ms McPhee was awarded £1,000 for
injury to feelings.

If employers are unaware of the harassment they may still be liable. However, if an employer can demonstrate that all reasonable practicable steps have been taken to prevent the harassment, then this may serve as a defence against liability.

TACKLING SEXUAL HARASSMENT

Ideally, every employer, no matter how large or small the organisation, should have a published policy for dealing with problems of sexual harassment so that if employees are subjected to harassment they know who they can turn to and that the matter will be dealt with confidentially and sympathetically.

It is often assumed that sexual harassment only occurs between individuals of the opposite sex. This is not necessarily so and therefore a policy statement should take care to include provision for dealing with harassment by men towards men and women towards women.

A successful harassment policy will provide for the following:

CONFIDENTIALITY

It is essential that throughout the whole issue the matter is treated with the utmost confidentiality. This extends beyond the counsellor involved with the victim and must include all those involved with the complaint as well as ensuring the safekeeping of any records that need to be kept.

COUNSELLORS

It is essential that employees are able to seek assistance from someone of their own sex who they can trust and who is accessible to them. The choice of counsellors is therefore vital in terms of their own personal credibility in the workplace as well as being seen to be approachable by all levels of staff. They should have good communication and listening skills.

Counsellors may be appointed from either the Personnel function or from a cross section of the workforce and should be representative of both sexes. The role of the counsellor would be:

- to provide a confidential sounding board to employees who believe that they are the victims of sexual harassment

- to offer support and sympathy and to help determine whether the behaviour complained of is harassment

- to help victims in deciding what action they wish to take and what they want to happen

- to understand the formal complaints procedure and to guide the employee towards taking the proper action towards resolving the problem.

Counsellors should be given the support of their management in being allowed the appropriate time to be able to carry out their counselling role and have access to suitable accommodation where they can hold meetings with victims in private.

Suitable training and guidance should be given so that counsellors fully understand their role and when they should seek further help and support from within the organisation or when they should recommend help from outside sources.

INFORMAL ACTION

Employees who feel that they are being harassed should first try to resolve the matter informally by telling the harasser that his or her behaviour is offensive and unwanted and that it must stop. If they are unable to do this face to face then they may prefer to give their message in writing.

They should be able to seek advice from their counsellor who would be available to give advice and support on how to tackle it.

FORMAL COMPLAINTS PROCEDURE

If the informal action has failed to put a stop to the harassment or if the harassment is of a more serious nature, then the formal complaints procedure should be invoked.

The employee should speak directly to his/her immediate supervisor or where this is not possible to the next level of management.

If employees find that the matter complained of is too embarassing, or it is too difficult to do this, then they should be able to ask their representative or their counsellor to act on their behalf.

Provision should be made to enable a female member of staff to take her complaint to a female manager or for a male member of staff to take his complaint to a male manager where this may be more appropriate.

Once a formal complaint has been made the employee should be required to record the details of his or her complaint in writing together with details of previous requests to the harasser to stop.

If the complaint results in a disciplinary hearing, then the employee must be willing to either give evidence at the hearing or provide a written statement detailing his or her complaint.

FOLLOW-UP ACTION BY MANAGEMENT

The supervisor or manager with whom the complaint has been raised should be responsible for ensuring that an investigation is carried out sensitively, discreetly and as quickly as possible.

It may be more appropriate for the investigation to be carried out by a more suitable designated person of the same sex as the employee who has brought the complaint. This person should not be the same person as the counsellor or representative of the victim but may be another trained counsellor unconnected with the case.

The supervisor or manager should be responsible for notifying the alleged harasser in writing that a complaint has been made so that the person complained about has the opportunity of putting forward his or her side of the case before any decision is taken as to whether the matter should be referred to a formal disciplinary hearing.

DISCIPLINARY HEARING

If it is decided that the matter should be referred to a disciplinary hearing then the normal Disciplinary Rules and Procedures should be applied. This means that:

- The alleged harasser should have sufficient notice of the date of the hearing to be able to prepare his or her case so that he or she may put forward any mitigating circumstances at the hearing.

- If they wish, the alleged harasser's representative should be allowed to attend the meeting but not take part in discussions unless requested to do so.

- Those responsible for hearing the complaint should ensure that the alleged harasser has every opportunity to state his or her side of the case and if necessary further investigations should be carried out before the outcome of the hearing is decided.

If appropriate, the alleged harasser should be given the opportunity of bringing witnesses to give statements, or, where this is not practicable, to provide written statements in support of his or her case.

The employee who has raised the complaint may be required to give evidence at the hearing or to submit written evidence of his or her complaint. In addition he or she may wish to provide witnesses to give statements or, as above, written statements in support of his or her complaint.

As stated above, the employee should be allowed to have his or her counsellor or representative present who should not be permitted to take part in the discussions unless requested to do so.

Following the disciplinary hearing the action taken against the harasser will depend on the seriousness of the offence. For example, a minor offence could result in an oral warning being given whereas a very serious offence could result in summary dismissal.

If a warning is given, it should be made clear to the harasser that any future proven harassment or victimisation will be regarded as a very serious offence which could result in dismissal.

RIGHT OF APPEAL BY THE HARASSER

The person disciplined should have the right to appeal against the decision taken by following the normal Disciplinary Appeals Procedure.

The Disciplinary Appeals Procedure should state the time limit in which the appeal should be made and to whom. Normally the person to whom the appeal should be made will be more senior to the person responsible for taking the disciplinary decision and he or she should not have been involved in the matter before the appeal stage.

OUTCOME

The employee who raised the complaint should be notified in writing of the outcome of his or her complaint and what action, if any, has been taken against the alleged harasser.

TRANSFERRING EMPLOYEES FOLLOWING HARRASSMENT

When a complaint of harassment has been made, depending upon the seriousness of the offence, it may be difficult for the parties to continue to work in the same working area or department.

Failure to recognise and deal with this situation could lead to further stress and anxiety on the part of the victim. The difficulty then arises as to which employee should be the one to move.

If the complaint has been found to be unjustified then the matter would seem to be more clear cut in that the employee who has been complained about but has been found to be "innocent" cannot be expected to move against his or her will.

However, if the complaint is upheld then the problem may be more complex.

Ideally it should be the harasser who is required to accept a move away from his or her victim. However, the harasser may be more senior to his or her victim and it may be easier to find alternative work or a new workplace for the person who has been harassed. If this is acceptable to the employee then there is no problem with making suitable mutually acceptable new arrangements.

If it is not acceptable and the victim is not willing to move, the problem becomes more complex. If necessary, alternative working arrangements or working accommodation will need to be arranged for the harasser.

USEFUL ADDRESS

Equal Opportunities Commission
Overseas House
Quay Street
Manchester
M3 3HN

Telephone No. 061 833 9244

4 RACIAL HARASSMENT

WHAT IS MEANT BY RACIAL HARASSMENT?

Racial harassment is a hostile or offensive act or expression, based on race, by an individual or group of one racial or ethnic origin against an individual or group of another racial or ethnic origin.

Although Racial Harassment is not specifically defined in the Race Relations Act 1976, harassment on the grounds of race can amount to unlawful discrimination. If the complaint is not properly investigated and action, if appropriate, not taken against the harasser then an Industrial Tribunal may infer that unlawful discrimination has occurred.

Examples of racial harassment behaviour may include:

- Physical abuse or intimidation

- Abusive language, mockery, racist jokes

- Patronising remarks

- Racial name calling

 • Intrusive questioning about a person's racial or ethnic origin, culture or religion or subjecting this to mockery

- Display or circulation of racially offensive material, racist graffiti

- Unfair allocation of work and responsibilities

- Unfair pressure on employees about speed and quality of work

- Threatening behaviour to incite violence

●Exclusion from normal workplace conversation or social events

●Offensive comments about appearance or dress

Often, people will call other people by names which they will classify as camaraderie or simply leg-pulling. However, it can be difficult to determine what may be found to be offensive even if it is not intended as such. Much will depend upon the context in which the remarks have been made.

CASE STUDY

In De Souza v The Automobile Association, CA 1985, Mrs De Souza was employed as a secretary/ personal assistant when she overheard one manager say to another in respect of herself to get his typing done by "the wog".

The Court of Appeal held that a racial insult is not enough, by itself, to be a "detriment" within the meaning of the Race Relations Act even if the insult caused the employee distress. It would have to have been shown that she had suffered some disadvantage in the circumstances in which she had to work or that she had been treated less favourably by the person who had used the word, unless it had been intended that she should have overheard the conversation or that the insult would have been passed on to her.

THE EFFECTS OF RACIAL HARASSMENT IN THE WORKPLACE

REDUCED EFFICIENCY

If employees feel under anxiety or stress as a result of being harassed then their effectiveness will fall while their energies and efforts are taken up with trying to cope with the unpleasantness of the situation. Output of work is bound to drop, more mistakes are likely to be made and accidents could happen.

CONFLICTS IN THE WORKPLACE

With sexual harassment personal conflict is more likely to be limited to an individual being harassed and to a lesser extent it may affect those immediately working around them.

Conflicts of a racial nature could lead to more widespread repercussions in an organisation, as others of the same or even other minority groups may regard the harassment not as being just against an individual but against their entire race, ethnic group or nationality thus leading to racial disharmony on a potentially large scale throughout an organisation. It could even lead to violence.

FINANCIAL COSTS

Time and money spent in defending claims together with the potential costs of compensation can be high in cases where the employer has failed to take action in a potential case of harassment.

At Industrial Tribunal the amount of compensation that may be awarded is up to a maximum amount set by the State and reviewed in April each year. The amount for the year 1993/94 is £11,000 including injury to feelings.

An employee may be able to claim for unfair dismissal where the potential maximum award may be as high as

- £6,150 basic award plus

- £11,000 compensatory award, including injury to feeling, plus

- £10,660 additional award for failing to re-engage or re-instate

- Common law claims pursued in the High Court are not limited by any maximum amount.

WHO IS LIABLE IN CASES OF RACIAL HARASSMENT?

The law allows for action to be taken against individual employees as well as the harasser's employer.

Employers are not only liable for their own actions but they can be held liable for the actions of their employees as well if they were made aware of the harassment and failed to take any steps to remedy it.

CASE STUDY

In Sutton v Balfour Beatty Construction, IT 1991, Mr Sutton worked on a construction site as a general labourer. Over a period of some 20 months the general foreman started abusing him by calling him a "black bastard".

Case Study (continued)

The site manager knew about the abuse but did nothing about it until Mr Sutton complained, following which he told the general foreman not to use such language.

Some months later Mr Sutton had a meeting with the industrial relations manager who appeared to suggest that the words "black bastard" could be treated as camaraderie and were not unusual in the construction industry.

The industrial tribunal did not accept that it was usual to call people who are black "black bastards" and strongly disapproved of any employers and particularly industrial relations managers who condoned such language. It was found that Mr Sutton had been less favourably treated on the grounds of his race and that the general foreman had subjected him to a detriment by abusing him with the words "black bastard". The company could not avoid liability for the general foreman's actions because it had failed to stop the general foreman from using such abusive language much sooner than it did. Mr Sutton was awarded compensation of £2,000 for injury to feelings.

If employers are unaware of the harassment they may still be liable. However, if it can be demonstrated that all reasonable steps were taken by the employer to prevent the harassment then this may serve as a defence against liability.

TACKLING RACIAL HARASSMENT

Employees who are subjected to harassment should know who they can turn to and that the matter will be dealt with sympathetically and in confidence. Ideally, every employer will have a published policy for dealing with such problems. It may be decided to incorporate all kinds of harassment and bullying in the same document although in some organisations it may be necessary for the policy to be more comprehensive to ensure that employees are not disadvantaged because of language difficulties or cultural misunderstandings.

It should not be assumed that harassment occurs only between individuals or groups of different cultural backgrounds. Harassment may occur between individuals or groups from the same background and the policy should allow for this possibility. For example, harassment may occur between two individuals or groups who are all West Indian or all Afro Caribbean in which case it may be more appropriate to follow the steps described for dealing with bullying. The policies for dealing with bullying and harassment will inevitably follow similar principles and it may be decided to incorporate them into one policy.

A successful harassment policy will provide for the following:

CONFIDENTIALITY

All those involved with the complaint, including the counsellor, should ensure that the matter is dealt with in complete confidence.

Any records which it is felt necessary to keep should be kept in a safe place.

COUNSELLORS

Employees should be able to seek assistance from someone who, if at all possible, understands their culture and if required, is of the same sex. They should possess a high level of credibility in the workplace as well as being approachable and accessible to all levels of staff. They should have good communication and listening skills. It may be that the counsellors will be the same as for sexual harassment.

If there are language difficulties then the employee should be offered the opportunity of bringing a work colleague or even a friend or relative from outside the organisation to meetings to assist with translations.

Counsellors may be appointed from either the Personnel function or from a cross-section of the workforce and should, where possible, be representative of the different cultures and from both sexes.
The role of the counsellors would be:

- to provide a confidential sounding board to employees who believe that they are the victims of racial harassment

- to offer support and sympathy and to help determine whether the behaviour complained of is harassment

- to help the victim decide what action he or she wishes to take and what he or she wants to happen

- to understand the formal complaints procedure and to guide the employee towards taking the proper action towards resolving the problem.

Counsellors should be given the support of their management in being allowed the appropriate time to be able to carry out their counselling role and have access to suitable accommodation where they can hold meetings with victims in private.

Suitable training and guidance should be given so that counsellors fully understand their role. They should know where to seek further help and support from within the organisation and be familiar with the bodies that exist outside the organisation which might be able to give further assistance such as the Equal Opportunities Commission or the Commission for Racial Equality.

INFORMAL ACTION

If employees feel that they are being harassed, they should first try to resolve the matter informally by telling the harasser that his or her behaviour is giving offence and that it must stop. If they are unable to do this face to face they may prefer to give their message in writing.

They should be able to seek advice from their counsellor who would be available to give advice and support on how to tackle it.

FORMAL COMPLAINTS PROCEDURE

If the informal action has failed to put a stop to the harassment or if the harassment is of a more serious nature, then the formal complaints procedure should be invoked.

The employee should speak directly to his or her immediate supervisor or, where this is not possible, to the next level of management.

If employees find that the matter complained of is too embarassing or it is too difficult to do this or where there may be a difficulty in communicating because of language difficulties then they should be able to ask for their representative or their counsellor to act on their behalf.

Provision should be made to enable a female member of staff to take her complaint to a female manager or for a male member of staff to take his complaint to a male manager.

If there are language difficulties then arrangements should be made for a mutually acceptable person to attend to assist with translating the discussions.

Once a formal complaint has been made the employee should be required to record the details of his or her complaint in writing together with details of previous requests to the harasser to stop. As above, if there are language difficulties then appropriate assistance should be provided.

If the complaint results in a disciplinary hearing then the employer must be willing to either give evidence at the hearing or provide a written statement detailing his or her complaint.

FOLLOW-UP ACTION BY MANAGEMENT

The supervisor or manager with whom the complaint has been raised should be responsible for ensuring that an investigation is carried out sensitively, discreetly and as quickly as possible.

It may be more appropriate for the investigation to be carried out by a more suitable designated person of the same cultural background as the person who has brought the complaint. This person should not be the same person as the counsellor or representative of the victim but may be another trained counsellor unconnected with the case.

The supervisor or manager should be responsible for notifying the alleged harasser in writing that a complaint has been made so that the person complained about has the opportunity of putting forward his or her side of the case before any decision is taken as to whether the matter should be referred to a formal disciplinary hearing.

DISCIPLINARY HEARING

If it is decided that the matter should be referred to a disciplinary hearing then the normal Disciplinary Rules and Procedures should be applied. This means that:

- The alleged harasser should have sufficient notice of the date of the hearing to be able to prepare his or her case so that he or she may put forward any mitigating circumstances at the hearing.

- If they wish, both the alleged harasser's representative and the victim's representative should be allowed to attend the meeting but not take part in discussions unless requested to do so by the person conducting the hearing.

- Those responsible for hearing the complaint should ensure that the alleged harasser has every opportunity to state his or her side of the case and if necessary further investigations should be carried out before the outcome of the hearing is decided.

If appropriate, the alleged harasser should be given the opportunity of bringing witnesses to give statements, or where this is not practicable, to provide written witness statements in support of his or her case.

The employee who has raised the complaint may be required to give evidence at the hearing or to submit written evidence of his or her complaint. In addition he or she may wish to provide witnesses to give statements or, as above, written statements, in support of his or her complaint.

As stated above the employee should be allowed to have his or her representative present or if preferred his or her counsellor.

Following the disciplinary hearing the action taken against the harasser will depend upon the seriousness of the offence. For example a minor offence could result in an oral warning being given whereas a very serious offence could result in summary dismissal.

If a warning is given it should be made clear to the harasser that any future proven harassment or victimisation will be regarded as a very serious offence which could result in dismissal.

RIGHT OF APPEAL BY THE HARASSER

The person disciplined should have the right of appeal against the decision taken by following the normal Disciplinary Appeals Procedure.

The Disciplinary Appeals Procedure should state the time limit in which the appeal should be made and to whom. Normally the person to whom the appeal should be made will be more senior to the person responsible for taking the disciplinary decision nor should he or she have been involved in the matter before the appeal stage.

OUTCOME

The employee who raised the complaint should be notified in writing of the outcome of his or her complaint and what action, if any, has been taken against the alleged harasser.

TRANSFERRING EMPLOYEES FOLLOWING HARASSMENT

When a complaint of racial harassment has been made, depending upon the seriousness of the offence, it may be difficult for the parties to continue to work in the same area or department.

Similarly, a failure to recognise and deal with this situation could lead to further stress and anxiety on the part of the victim. As before, the difficulty then arises as to which employee should be the one to move.
The principles to follow would be as before, ie:

- If the complaint is unfounded then the employee who has been complained about but has been found to be "innocent" cannot be expected to move against his or her will.

- If the complaint has been upheld then ideally it should be the harasser who is required to accept a move away from his or her victim.

- If the harasser is the more senior employee then it may be difficult to find alternative work or a new workplace, in which case the victim may be willing to make the change. If this is acceptable then there is no problem.

- If the victim is unwilling to move then it may be necessary for alternative working arrangements or working accommodation to be organised for the harasser.

An employee cannot be required to move to a new workplace or new location against his or her will unless there is a specific clause in the contract of employment allowing the employer to make such changes. To force an employee to move without his or her agreement would amount to a breach of contract.

If the harasser does refuse to accept a move and the employer believes that to continue his or her employment under the existing arrangements will create insurmountable difficulties then the employer would have to terminate the harasser's existing contract and offer alternative arrangements if any are available.

If the offer is rejected then the employee would be dismissed. If the employee submitted a claim for unfair dismissal it would be up to the employer to defend the decision to dismiss based on the reasons and reasonableness of his or her actions.

USEFUL ADDRESS

Commission for Racial Equality
Elliott House
10–12 Allington Street
London
SW1E 5EM

Telephone No. 071 828 7022

RELIGIOUS OBSERVANCE IN THE WORKPLACE

THE BRITISH TRADITION

The standard working week in the UK, Monday to Friday, was, not surprisingly, originally structured to accommodate the majority culture ie the Christian faith. In addition, the majority of our public holidays are linked to Christian festivals, for example Christmas, Easter and Whitsun. Even though many Christians do not attend church on a regular basis or observe many of the Christian festivals, the traditional working arrangements are still in place to enable those who are practising Christians to follow their religion without experiencing conflicting loyalties in the workplace.

Sunday and public holiday working is not a normal requirement for most employers although in recent years there has been an increasing trend for some of the major supermarket chains and "do it yourself" shops and stores to open seven days a week with the exception of certain public holidays such as Christmas Day.

CHANGES IN OUR SOCIETY

There are now many religions and sects represented in our multi-cultural and multi-faith society. This means that holy days and religious festivals are celebrated throughout the year as well as prayer meetings which are held during the day as well as on a weekly basis.

LEGAL IMPLICATIONS

The Fair Employment (Northern Ireland) Act 1989 makes it unlawful to discriminate either directly or indirectly on grounds of religious belief or political opinion.

In the rest of the UK there is no law which protects people from discrimination on similar grounds although discrimination on the grounds of race is unlawful under the Race Relations Act 1976. It is therefore important to be able to distinguish which religious groups may also be recognised as ethnic groups.

The House of Lords have set down the following guidelines:

- There must be a long shared history of which the group is conscious as distinguishing it from other groups and the memory of it which keeps it alive.

- There must be a cultural tradition of its own including family and social customs often but not necessarily associated with religious observance.

Other characteristics which may be relevant include:

- A common geographical origin or a descent from a small number of common ancestors

- A common language not necessarily peculiar to the group

  A common literature peculiar to the group

  A common religion different from that of neighbouring groups or from the general community surrounding it

- Being a minority or being an oppressed or dominant group within a larger community.

Using the above criteria the House of Lords has ruled that Sikhs are a racial group defined by ethnic origins and are therefore entitled to protection under the provisions of the Race Relations Act.

Contrary to that, EAT has taken the view in Crown Suppliers (PSA) v Dawkins (EAT 1989) that Rastafarians, although a religious group, are not an "ethnic group" because their 60 year old history was not long enough to set them apart from the rest of the Afro-Caribbean community.

This meant that Mr Dawkins, who was refused a job as a driver because of his distinctive rastafarian hairstyle, was unable to make a complaint by invoking the provisions of the Race Relations Act.

This case has gone to appeal and therefore this decision may be overturned.

The position of Muslims has not been considered by the EAT and Tribunals have come up with differing opinions.

TIME OFF WORK

Whereas most employees who are practising Christians will find that they are not required to work on the occasions that they wish to attend church, employees of other faiths may well find that their religious festivals and regular days of worship fall within the normal working time prescribed by their employers. This may give rise to conflict between the employees' requirement to take time off and the employers' need to have their employees in place to cope with the operational needs of the business.

Employees of the same religion may themselves have different requirements for time off depending upon their degree of religious observance. For example, an organisation which employs Jews may well find that many are quite prepared to work normally after sunset on a Friday while others may be totally inflexible because of the level of their observance.

Many employers are now much more flexible in their approach and will do their utmost to be accommodating by adjusting working hours or allowing employees to swop shifts. In conflicts such as this the courts will look to see whether the employers' needs are justifiable and whether any attempts to find an amicable solution have been made. They will also take into account the size and resources of the organisation.

CASE STUDY

In the Post Office v Mayers, Mr Mayers was employed to load post at a station. He had worked regular Mondays to Fridays for 20 years when he was transferred to permanent late shifts ending at 11.00 pm at night. Mr Mayers was a member of the Worldwide Church of God which prohibited its members from working on the Sabbath which ran from sunset on Fridays until sunset on Saturdays.

He initially used up his annual leave and then took unauthorised leave to get round having to leave work early on Fridays. He was offered the opportunity of working a four and a half day week with his pay reduced pro-rata which he refused. He was subsequently disciplined and eventually dismissed for misconduct after continuing to leave early on Fridays.

The EAT upheld the dismissal on the basis that the employer had taken reasonable steps to find a solution but Mr Mayers had not been prepared to compromise. EAT also referred to a Court of Appeal decision where it was stated that an employee is not entitled to absent himself or herself from work for the purpose of religious observance if that absence was in breach of the contract of employment.

PRAYING DURING WORKING TIME

There are certain religions which require prayers to be said during the course of the day and some employers, where space permits, will provide a prayer room for use either on an individual basis and/or for communal use. Provision of such a room will minimise the disruption which could be caused if employees would otherwise need to leave the premises to meet their religious requirements.

For example the faith of Islam requires the practice of four obligatory daily prayers:

- Dawn (Fajr) – to be said at any time between the first light of dawn and sunrise, generally for a period of about one hour

- Early afternoon (Zuhr) – to be said at any time between immediately after midday and mid-afternoon. On Fridays this prayer is replaced by the compulsory communal prayer (Jumua)

- Late afternoon (Asr) – to be said at any time between mid-afternoon and the beginning of dusk although it is preferable to say it in the earlier part of this period

- Sunset (Maghrib) – to be said during the period of dusk but preferably just after sunset.

All prayers require a state of cleanliness which may mean that a ritual of washing the face, forearms, hands and feet or a shower or bath with clean running water must be undertaken beforehand.

These prayers average between 10 and 20 minutes and together with the average of five minutes taken for washing can easily be fitted into the working day with a degree of flexibility and understanding from both the employer and the employee.

The timings for prayers are normally published well in advance by the various religious bodies so that it is possible to plan ahead to minimise disruption in the work-place. The exact timing of religious festivals may not always be possible until nearer the date as they are dependent upon the visibility of the moon and predicted dates can vary by up to a day.

DRESS AND APPEARANCE

Dress and appearance may cause problems because the requirements of the employer may conflict with the religious dress rules of employees.

Many employers require their employees to wear a uniform at work which may consist simply of an overall or other "over garment" or may include all outer garments, for example shirts, blouses, ties, scarves, trousers, skirts, shoes and even jackets and overcoats or raincoats.

As with working hours, employers are becoming much more flexible in their approach and are willing to accommodate an employee's religious dress requirements either by adapting the uniform or allowing greater flexibility. For example, a range of uniforms may be available to cater for the different religious requirements or clothing may have to be of a pre-determined colour but in any reasonable style.

If a uniform is provided purely to create a corporate image then it may be difficult to convince the courts that it is a justifiable requirement. In Malik v British Home Stores Mrs Malik, a Muslim, was prohibited from wearing trousers rather than a skirt under the overall which was worn by all female shop assistants. The Tribunal held that the detriment to Muslims far outweighed the commercial necessity of imposing such a requirement.

If an employer is not prepared to be flexible then the rules laid down must be justifiable on grounds of business need or to meet health and safety requirements.

CASE STUDY

In Panesar v The Nestle Co Ltd, Mr Panesar was refused employment because he had a beard and beards were prohibited in the factory for hygiene reasons. EAT dismissed his claim that he had been indirectly discriminated against despite the fact that other factories may allow the wearing of snoods over beards and held that the refusal to allow beards in the factory was justifiable.

By contrast, in Bhakherd v Famous Names Limited, Mr Blakherd, a Sikh, was unable to wear the hat provided by his employer because of his turban. The Tribunal found that the requirement to wear a hat was unjustifiable because turbans are washable, completely cover the hair and were adequate if not better than the hat provided by the company for the purposes of hygiene.

An exception has been incorporated into UK legislation which enables Sikhs who work on construction sites and who would normally be required by law to wear a safety helmet be allowed instead to wear a turban. Because of this exception neither the Sikh nor the employer would be liable in tort for any injury, loss or damage caused by a failure to comply with the legal requirements for construction workers to wear safety helmets.

Anyone causing injury, loss or damage to a Sikh which

can be attributed to the fact that he was not wearing a safety helmet will only be liable to the extent that he would have suffered loss, damage or injury if he had been wearing a helmet. The same principle would apply in the event of death.

CATERING ARRANGEMENTS

Religious rules may mean that the typical national dishes such as pork chops or steak and kidney pudding produced in a staff canteen may not meet the dietary requirements of different religious or ethnic groups.

For example, Muslims and Jews are both prohibited from eating pork or any other products from the pig and other meat which they are allowed to eat must be slaughtered in a prescribed manner ie the Halal process for Muslims and the Jewish Kosher process for Jews.

It may be that some employers are big enough and have sufficient resources to be able to provide a range of meals prepared in such a way that the religious rules of their employees are complied with. Where this is not practicable it should be possible to provide a range of vegetarian options which meet the requirements of both religious observance and vegetarians.

ACCOMMODATING THE VARIOUS RELIGIONS IN THE WORKPLACE

It is important to ensure that employees do not feel that any one religious group is being treated more favourably than another with regard to its beliefs being respected or that one particular group is affecting the earnings potential of others because of time spent away from the place of work.

By discussing the problems and their possible solutions with employees, their staff representatives or their trade union representatives it should be possible in many instances to accommodate the requirements of employees' various religious beliefs without causing disruption or animosity in the workplace.

Depending upon the nature of the work processes, it may be possible to allow working hours to be adapted or to allow additional time off to be taken without pay provided that manning levels remain at a suitable level at any one time to ensure that the operational requirements of the business are maintained satisfactorily.

PERSONAL RELATIONSHIPS

In most organisations it is not unusual for personal relationships to develop between members of staff and in the majority of instances this is of no concern to the employer

Problems can occur, however, when the relationship affects the employer's business, for example:

DISCLOSURE OF CONFIDENTIAL INFORMATION

If an employee establishes a relationship with a partner who is employed with a competitor or even in the same organisation and there is a genuine risk that the disclosure of confidential information could be seriously harmful to the employee's business then dismissal of the person not entitled to access to such information may be seen to be fair.

CASE STUDY

In Dyer v Inverclyde Taxis Limited, both Mr and Mrs Dyer were employed by the same Taxi Owners Association. Mrs Dyer was employed as a Cashier/ Secretary and her husband was employed as a Manager and as the owner of two taxis. Mr Dyer was made redundant and subsequently moved his two taxis to a rival organisation. As a result of this Mrs Dyer was dismissed for "some other substantial reason" on the grounds that she would have access to confidential information which, if passed on to her husband, would seriously harm her employer's business.

> **Case Study** (continued)
>
> Even though Mrs Dyer's evidence that she had not given, nor had it entered her head to give, any company information to her husband after he had been dismissed was accepted, the EAT supported the Tribunal's view that the employer had acted fairly in taking steps to eliminate a risk in an area which was vital to the success of its operation.

PERSONAL RELATIONSHIPS AT WORK

Frequently when a relationship develops, one of the couple may have responsibility for the other. This may not cause a problem while everything runs smoothly but matters can easily go wrong. For example, one may cover up for the other's mistakes, others in the work group may feel that there is favouritism particularly when salaries are reviewed or when there are opportunities for advancement or for interesting assignments to be allocated.

Many employers do not permit married couples or couples in close relationships to work for each other. Where such rules exist they should be clearly stated so that employees are aware that one member of the couple may be required to move to an alternative position or location, or may be required to leave if no suitable alternative is available for him or her.

The rules may provide for the more junior member of the couple to be the one required to move unless an opportunity exists for the senior of the two to move. If the requirement to move was based on the assumption that it should always be the female, or that it should always be the male, of the partnership, then this could amount to sex discrimination.

Many organisations will not permit fathers, mothers, sons and daughters to work in a situation where one is responsible for the other. Where this is the case it should be clearly stated in the recruitment policy so that those responsible for recruitment of staff both from external and internal sources as well as the employees themselves are aware of the rules.

EMPLOYEES' PERSONAL CONDUCT

Occasionally, relationships may affect the way an individual behaves in the workplace. For example, in the case where an employee is infatuated with another, significant time may be lost in day dreaming or spent talking to each other with the inevitable deterioration in work performance.

If the infatuation is one-sided, problems may occur with both parties. On the one hand, difficulties may arise with the person who is being rejected, which may manifest itself in the standard of work performance suffering. It may even create problems with other personal relationships in the working environment.

If this results in the deterioration of an employee's effectiveness then it may be necessary first to counsel the employee or offer advice on where further counselling may be sought. If this does not have the desired effect then it may be necessary to consider taking disciplinary action in an endeavour to resolve the matter.

The person who is being pursued but is not interested may feel that he or she is being harassed. If he or she is unable to stop the harassment by letting the harasser know that the behaviour is not wanted then he or she should be able to pursue his or her complaint by following the Harassment Policy.

PARTICULAR DIFFICULTIES WITH EMPLOYING COUPLES

One of the difficulties in employing a couple in a small team or company is going to be that they will most likely want to take leave at the same time.

This may create enormous work coverage problems and it may in itself be sufficient reason to require one member of the couple to move to another department or work location or, where this is not possible, to dismiss.

Another problem which may occur when employing couples is when one partner is dismissed for misconduct and the company loses confidence and trust in the remaining partner. However, for the dismissal to be upheld as fair an organisation would need to be able to demonstrate that the loss of confidence and trust were as a result of the dismissed employee's actions and not based on assumptions because of his or her relationship with a third party.

CASE STUDY

In Wadley v Eager Electrical Limited, Mrs Wadley, who was employed as a shop assistant, was dismissed for misappropriating company money. Shortly afterwards, Mr Wadley who was employed by the same company as a service engineer was also dismissed, even though he had 17 years' service with a good track record and there was no more than a suspicion of his involvement in the theft. The EAT decided that it can only be the act of either the employer or employee that can breach the mutual obligation of trust and confidence and that Mrs Wadley's conduct could not have breached that duty as far as her husband was concerned.

EMPLOYING COUPLES TO WORK AS A TEAM

There are many instances where couples are employed to work as a team and are jointly employed under a joint contract of employment. Typical examples are pubs, hotels or clubs where it is a condition of their employment that if one of the partners leaves for whatever reason then the remaining partner cannot continue to be employed. Dismissal of the remaining partner would be for "some other substantial reason".

CASE STUDY

In Provins & Provins v Martin the Newsagent Limited, both Mr and Mrs Provins were employed and were provided with live in accommodation. It was decided that Mr Provins had been fairly dismissed for capability and his wife was fairly dismissed for "some other substantial reason", because although there was no complaint against her it was accepted that their two employments were dependent upon their both remaining in the employment of Martin.

If a couple is employed in joint employment but on separate contracts it will be much harder to claim that the two employments stand or fall together or to dismiss a partner for "some other substantial reason" following the termination of employment of the other partner.

CASE STUDY

In Great Mountain and Tumble Rugby Football Club v Howlett, there was a written agreement stating that Mr and Mrs Howlett were employed on the basis of a joint appointment as a husband and wife team and that notice given by either would terminate the agreement and subsequently both their employments.

Mr Howlett who was employed as the steward was dismissed when his wife resigned from her employment after they had had a row. As Mrs Howlett's duties were minimal in that she occasionally helped out behind the bar and that her absence would not have made a substantial difference, the Industrial Tribunal deemed the dismissal to be unfair.

MOVING EMPLOYEES TO ALTERNATIVE WORKPLACES

In many of the above instances it has been suggested that the solution may be to move one of the partners in a relationship to either a new department or section, or to a new location.

However, it should be borne in mind that one cannot simply transfer or relocate an employee against his or her will unless there is provision in the contract of employment allowing the employer to make such changes. To force an employee to move against his or her wishes would amount to a breach of contract.

If an employee does refuse to accept a move and the employer truly believes that employment under the existing arrangements cannot be allowed to continue because of genuine business difficulties, then the employer would have to terminate the employee's existing contract and offer the alternative work that was available.

If the offer is rejected then the employee would be dismissed and it would be up to him or her to make a claim for unfair dismissal. It would then be down to the employers to defend the decision to dismiss based on the reasons and reasonableness of their actions on the grounds of "some other substantial reason".

HIV AND AIDS

AIDS is a major health hazard which is unlikely to disappear in the foreseeable future, and the numbers of cases reported are on the increase. In the UK, by the end of June 1992, nearly 18,000 people were known to be infected with the HIV virus although the actual number is assumed to be much higher. Over half of these were known to be homosexuals. 6,000 people were reported as having AIDS, over half of whom have died. There has been a 37% increase in known cases of heterosexuals developing AIDS.

From these statistics, it follows that many employers can expect to have employees on their staff with either HIV or AIDS.

One of the biggest problems facing employers is the lack of knowledge and understanding about HIV and AIDS. This means that many employees who are infected suffer from discriminatory and insensitive practices arising from their colleagues' fears and suspicions which are largely due to ignorance of the facts.

Employers can take steps to prevent this happening by providing information and establishing policies to deal with such issues. As with most situations, it is much easier to develop a policy before a problem arises so that emotions and personalities do not get in the way of sensible principles.

WHAT DO HIV AND AIDS MEAN?

Human Immunodeficiency Virus (HIV) is a virus which infects humans. Once an individual becomes infected with the virus he or she will carry it for ever. There is currently no known cure and therefore it cannot, at present, be eradicated from the body.

Infected persons may be unaware that they have the virus and will normally feel well although they may suffer from mild symptoms such as weight loss or enlarged glands.

After carrying the virus for a number of years, sometimes for up to ten or twelve years, some carriers of HIV will develop related illnesses known as the Acquired Immunodeficiency Syndrome (AIDS). This period of time is likely to increase as developments in delaying progression of the disease improve.

AIDS is the result of HIV affecting the immune system of the body. The immune system normally protects the human body from infections but with AIDS this system is partly destroyed, leaving the body susceptible to infections that would normally be harmless.

There is also a susceptibility to certain types of cancer, for example a rare skin cancer called Kaposi's Sarcoma, or a virulent form of pneumonia called Pneumocystis Carinae Pneumonia, which would normally be protected by the immune system.

There is usually no outward sign in the early stages that a person has AIDS although he or she will suffer from more severe infections than normally. With improved medical care sufferers are often only ill for short periods of time and are otherwise perfectly capable of working as usual. However, as the immune system becomes further destroyed, the infections will get more frequent and be harder to treat until eventually the sufferer may be unable to continue to work.

AIDS appears to be invariably fatal and usually results in death within a couple of years of contracting the disease although advances in medical knowledge are being made all the time.

HOW IS HIV PASSED ON?

The HIV virus cannot be transmitted to others from normal social or work contact. For example, according to medical advice, it *cannot* be passed on by:

- sharing toilet or washing facilities

- using the same crockery or towels

- handling food

- coughing, crying, sneezing or kissing

- insect bites

The infection *is* passed on by the mixing of body fluids in the following ways:

- homosexual or heterosexual intercourse with an infected person

- receiving infected blood transfusions or other infected blood products

- exposure to infected blood eg where needles or hypodermic syringes are shared with an infected person

- from an infected mother to her baby

Other than in health care environments there are few jobs which are likely to have any contact with infected blood or other body fluids.

Qualified first aiders should have been trained to take precautionary measures as a matter of routine when administering first aid, but all employees should be informed as part of the organisation's health and safety policy how to take the proper precautions in case they have to go to someone's assistance in an emergency.

WHO CAN BECOME INFECTED WITH HIV?

Initially it was principally homosexuals, haemophiliacs and injecting drug users. However heterosexuals are increasingly becoming infected with the virus and, as stated above, the true statistics are not known.

LEGAL IMPLICATIONS

HIV and AIDS are not notifiable diseases under the Public Health (Control of Disease) Act, therefore there is no requirement for employers to report such cases to the health authorities.

There is currently no British law which protects people who are infected with HIV or who have AIDS from discrimination although existing employment legislation has implications for issues such as:

- Medical tests
- Breach of confidentiality
- Discrimination
- Pressure from colleagues or company clients
- Dismissal on grounds of HIV
- Incapability dismissals

MEDICAL TESTS

Many employers already require prospective employees to undergo a medical examination or to submit a medical report from their general practitioner before an offer of employment is confirmed. To extend this to include

testing for HIV would be lawful provided that it did
not amount to unlawful sex or race discrimination. An
employer would be legally entitled to refuse employment
to a person who tested HIV positive without being
required to give that person any reason for the decision.

It should be remembered that under the Access to
Medical Reports Act 1988 employers are not entitled to
receive confidential medical reports without the written
consent of the individual.

An employer who wishes to introduce HIV testing for
existing employees will also need to have the consent of
the employee both to undergo the test and to allow the
results to be disclosed to the employer.

It is unlikely that an employer would be able to
claim that there was an implied term in the contract
of employment enabling him or her to require existing
employees to undergo HIV testing unless there was
reasonable cause to suspect that a particular employee
might pose a health risk to colleagues or members of the
public. For example, it might be justified if an employee's
job required him or her to travel abroad to countries
where they would be required to produce evidence of an
HIV negative test.

It should also be borne in mind that there is an implied
term of mutual trust and confidence in the contract of
employment of every employee. If an employer required
his or her employees to undergo such tests without
an express term existing in the contract then it would
probably be seen as a fundamental breach of the implied
term of trust and confidence leaving the way open for the
employee to resign and claim constructive dismissal.

It should be recognised that HIV testing has its
limitations in that it does not reveal the antibodies in the
blood during the first few months of becoming infected
nor whether an individual will eventually develop AIDS.

BREACH OF CONFIDENTIALITY

As with any other medical information or personal information that may be disclosed to an employer, either by the employee or with the permission of the employee, such information must be treated as confidential. Any records that are kept should be stored securely so that they cannot be accessed by unauthorised persons.

Under the Data Protection Act employees are entitled to see and validate information about themselves which is held on computer. The Act also prohibits the unauthorised disclosure of this information.

One of the implied terms in any contract of employment is the duty of trust and confidence between the parties. This means that if an employer discloses information about the employee, for example that an individual is infected with HIV/AIDS, without his or her agreement, then the employee could resign and claim constructive dismissal.

DISCRIMINATION

It is not unlawful to refuse to employ people who are infected with HIV or have AIDS. However, such discrimination could be attributed to sex or race discrimination.

Direct discrimination occurs when a person is treated less favourably than a person of the opposite sex/race would have been.

Indirect discrimination occurs when an employer imposes a requirement or condition which cannot be justified on grounds of sex/race and with which only a smaller proportion of one sex/race can comply and therefore the person suffers a detriment because he or she cannot comply.

For example, it could be unlawful direct race discrimination if an employer will not employ black people from African countries because AIDS is prevalent in those countries.

Similarly, if an employer refuses to employ homosexuals in certain capacities then, unless there are genuine health and safety grounds for not doing so, this could amount to direct sex discrimination.

PRESSURE FROM COLLEAGUES OR CLIENTS

Employers are often faced with pressure from other employees or even clients who refuse to work with an individual who is infected with HIV/AIDS.

Unless there is a genuine health and safety risk to colleagues then it is unlikely to be seen as a fair reason for dismissing the infected individual because of peer pressure.

Employers should try to help their employees to gain an understanding of the implications of HIV/AIDS by providing information and consultation so that their fears and suspicions are alleviated.

If employees persist in unreasonably refusing to work with their infected colleague then it may be necessary to give disciplinary warnings, which could ultimately lead to dismissal.

There may be situations where it may not be practicable to dismiss employees for refusing to work with their infected colleague for example if this would create widespread disruption in the workplace. Under these circumstances the employer may be left with little choice but to transfer or dismiss the infected employee and a Tribunal would take this into consideration when deciding if an employer had acted reasonably under all the circumstances.

As with pressure from colleagues, if an employer is under pressure from clients who threaten to remove their business, then the first step would be to try to consult with the clients about their concerns and if possible provide them with medical information in an attempt to gain their understanding and resolve their objections.

If this fails then the employer may have no alternative but to transfer the infected employee to where he or she has no contact with the client or to dismiss. Although the dismissal may be unjustified in principle, a Tribunal is likely to consider the decision fair as an employer may feel that he or she has no alternative but to protect the interests of the business if it is threatened in this way.

DISMISSAL ON GROUNDS OF HIV OR AIDS

Dismissal purely on the grounds that an employee was HIV positive or had AIDS is unlikely to be seen as a "fair" reason for dismissal.

DISMISSAL ON ILL-HEALTH GROUNDS

It may be that dismissal would be fair for reasons of "capability" or ill health.

Normally, if an employee is HIV positive or he or she develops AIDS, his or her ability to perform his or her job is unaffected. The difficulty arises when the employee becomes ill and is unable to attend work for either short or long periods at a time.

Under these circumstances the employee should be treated in exactly the same as any other employee who is suffering from ill-health, whether it be for long term or short term sickness absences.

CASE STUDY

In East Lindsay District Council v Daubney, EAT 1977, Mr Daubney was employed as a Surveyor. Following a mild stroke he was off sick for several months during which time the Personnel Director asked the District Community Physician whether he thought he ought to be retired on ill-health grounds. After an examination it was reported that Mr Daubney should be retired and he was subsequently dismissed.

Unfortunately at no time was Mr Daubney consulted prior to his dismissal although efforts had been made to obtain medical advice, and this led to a finding of unfair dismissal. This was not because the reasons were not justified but because the employer had not carried out sufficient investigations.

Following this, the Employment Appeals Tribunal (EAT) laid down the following guidelines which employers must observe when dealing with long-term sickness:

- Appropriate steps should be taken to determine the true medical position of the employee: this will normally involve seeking permission from the employee to obtain a medical report from his or her general practitioner.

- A further medical report should be obtained from an independent medical adviser if the employee requests it.

- The employee should be consulted prior to any decision being made in case there are any further facts which need to be considered before a decision is reached.

•Consideration should be given to offering the employee more suitable alternative work or even reduced hours where this is possible.

As stated earlier, an employee cannot be forced to give his or her consent to a medical report being obtained by the company and if this occurs it may be necessary to advise the employee that a decision will have to be made in the absence of information which could have a bearing on the outcome of the decision.

Short term persistent absences tend to be more disruptive to working arrangements in that the employer never knows when the next period of absence will occur. Because of this the courts take the view that there is only so much that an employer can be expected to put up with and provided that the employee has been given warnings then dismissal because of frequent absences will be considered to be a justifiable reason for dismissal.

If there is no medical evidence to support frequent self-certificated absences then the employee should be asked to consult his or her general practitioner to find out whether medical treatment is necessary and to give a prognosis about future illhealth.

In most instances where short term absences occur it would be a waste of time seeking a medical opinion if there is no common link between the illnesses.

CASE STUDY

In International Sports Co Ltd v Thomson, Mrs Thomson was employed as a racquet stringer. Mrs Thomson, whose level of absenteeism was significantly higher than other employees in organisation, had submitted medical certificates for dizzy

> **Case Study** (continued)
> spells, anxiety and nerves, bronchitis, virus infection, cystitis, dyspepsia and flatulence. Despite being given a number of warnings, Mrs Thomson's absenteeism record remained high. When the company doctor was consulted he gave the opinion that no useful purpose would be served by seeing Mrs Thomson because the illnesses were unrelated and there was therefore nothing that could be subsequently verified. The EAT agreed with the company doctor that all that could be established was that Mrs Thomson would have recovered by the time she returned to work and that it would be almost impossible to give any view about future sicknesses.

EAT have subsequently laid down the following guidelines that:

- A fair review of the absences should take place

- The employee should be given appropriate warnings that the level of attendance must improve.

Then if the absences persisted the employer would be justified in dismissing.

If an employer suspects that an employee is infected with HIV or has AIDS then a medical investigation may determine whether any help could be given the employee. Individuals who are infected are known to have more difficulty than usual in coping with stress which may account for much of their absences from work. It may be that re-arranging working hours or responsibilities may reduce stress and subsequently improve their capability to attend work.

COPING WITH HIV/AIDS IN THE WORKPLACE

A policy document setting out both the organisation's attitude towards people who are infected with HIV or have AIDS and the principles and procedures which should be followed should be made available to all employees. Line management responsible for staff matters should also be briefed so that they can deal with issues that may arise confidently and be able to answer difficult questions either from the infected person or their work colleagues.

The following may be included in a policy statement:

CONFIDENTIALITY

If it becomes known that an employee is infected with HIV or has AIDS then strict confidentiality must be maintained by the organisation. Any breaches of confidentiality will be treated as a disciplinary offence.

Any records which are necessary to be kept should be secured in a safe place.

Employees will not be required to inform their employer that they are sufferers although it may be helpful to the infected employee to advise the employer if his or her condition gives rise to periods of absence due to ill health so that where possible assistance can be provided for the employee.

If it is thought necessary to disclose the infected person's condition to any other employees then his or her written consent to the disclosure should first be obtained.

EMPLOYMENT POLICIES

RECRUITMENT

Medical evidence states that people who are infected with HIV or have AIDS present no risk of passing on the virus to others and should therefore be treated in exactly the same way as other external or internal applicants.

Applicants and existing employees should not be required to take a medical test for HIV or AIDS other than in exceptional circumstances, for example where there is a genuine risk on health and safety grounds or where employees will be required to travel to countries which require a negative test statement to gain entry.

Likewise medical questionnaires which prospective employees are asked to complete should not include questions asking if they have been tested for HIV and if so what the result was as this may discourage them from taking a test and seeking help if it is needed.

CONTINUED EMPLOYMENT

No employee should be dismissed purely because he or she is infected with HIV or has AIDS.

Every effort should be made by the employer to help the sufferer remain in employment for as long as he or she continues to be able to work. If possible, duties should be changed or re-arranged to enable the employee to continue to cope. Hours of work could be adjusted where this is practicable.

SICKNESS ABSENCES

The normal rules for sickness absences should continue to apply to infected employees. If appropriate, medical opinion should be sought so that advice may be given on how best to alleviate problems at work for the employee and so help him or her to continue working effectively for as long as possible.

HARASSMENT OR DISCRIMINATION

If any employee is found to have harassed or acted in a discriminatory way towards an infected employee then he or she should be subject to appropriate disciplinary action in the same way as for sex, race or any other form of discrimination or harassment.

ADVICE AND INFORMATION

THE FACTS ABOUT HIV AND AIDS

Employees should be given written advice on what HIV and AIDS means and how it develops. It should be spelt out as to how it is contracted so that employees are advised both how to prevent putting themselves at risk and to understand that there is no risk to them in the workplace. The summary entitled "What does HIV and AIDS mean" at the beginning of this chapter may provide a useful guide for this purpose. The Employment Department has produced a booklet entitled "AIDS and the Work Place – A guide for employers" and this can be obtained free from Department of Employment offices.

Management training and Induction training should include elements which provide an understanding of HIV and AIDS and about the company's policy so that employees are properly informed and fears and prejudices addressed.

The subject of HIV and AIDS should be on staff meeting agendas so that employees have the opportunity of airing their views and concerns and having their questions answered.

Outside sources of information should be made available to employees so that if they wish contact can be made without the knowledge of the employer. A list of addresses is included at the end of this chapter.

TRAVELLING ABROAD

PRE-ENTRY HIV NEGATIVE TESTS

Some countries insist on pre-entry HIV negative tests before they will allow workers entry from abroad. If an employee is to be required to travel as part of his or her job then he or she should be advised of this requirement prior to accepting employment where this is known. If travel is to a country that requires a negative test statement it should be remembered that the test can only be carried out with the employee's consent. It is advisable that the test be carried out in the UK prior to travelling. Further details can be obtained from the Foreign and Commonwealth Office and the embassies of the countries through which the employee is expected to travel.

ADVICE TO TRAVELLERS

The following people are at greater risk from becoming infected with HIV:

- Homosexuals

- People who have sex with prostitutes

- People who have casual sexual relationships

- Drug users who share syringes and hypodermic needles

- People who receive injections from equipment that has not been adequately sterilised

- People who have blood transfusions where the blood is not checked for HIV/AIDS

Employees travelling abroad should be warned of the dangers of casual relationships and the risk of passing the infection on to their usual partner on their return home.

In some less developed countries, particularly in rural areas, syringes, needles and other medical equipment may not be adequately sterilised and blood may not be checked before it is used for transfusions. It may be necessary to provide emergency medical packs or make arrangements for a fast return to the UK should this be needed.

FIRST AID

Qualified first aiders will normally have been trained in how to take precautionary measures against the usual infections including HIV/AIDS when administering first aid, and regular refresher training should be provided to ensure that they are kept up to date with the latest developments.

However, it may be that other employees may come to the rescue in the event of an emergency and it is therefore essential that not only are appointed first aiders kept up to date but so are all other employees. There are two key issues which give particular cause for concern by people involved with administering first aid.

CUTS AND BLEEDING

First aiders should ensure that any cuts or abrasions to their own hands are adequately covered with waterproof dressings or by wearing rubber gloves before treating any individual and that hands are thoroughly washed with soap and water before and after administering treatment. This will protect against other common infections as well as AIDS.

If any blood has been spilt on to the first aider's skin it should be well washed with soap and water and thoroughly rinsed.

If large spillages of blood occur it is advisable that rubber gloves be worn and paper towels used to mop it up. The area should then be cleaned with diluted household bleach.

MOUTH TO MOUTH RESUSCITATION

There is no evidence to suggest that HIV or AIDS can be spread by giving mouth to mouth resuscitation or, as stated earlier, even by simple social contact such as coughing, crying, kissing or sneezing.

However, first aiders may prefer to use oral airways or face pieces when carrying out mouth to mouth resuscitation. Under these circumstances it is essential that the first aider is skilled at using these devices as they make it much harder to maintain effective respiration and because of their rigidity they may cause bleeding around the lips which in itself is a potential source of infection.

GROUP LIFE INSURANCE SCHEMES

Many employers provide group life insurance schemes as a benefit for their employees. Depending upon the nature of the scheme, the insurers may require personal details about the individuals who are to be covered by the scheme. Such information could only be provided with the consent of employees.

This would include information on whether the employee has been counselled or had a blood test relating to HIV or AIDS. An applicant whose test was positive would not be provided with life cover. Further advice can be obtained from the Association of British Insurers.

USEFUL ADDRESSES

Association of British Insurers
51 Gresham Street
London
EC2V 7HQ

Telephone 071 600 3333

Foreign and Commonwealth Office
Travel Enquiries Unit

Telephone 071 270 4129

National AIDS Helpline

Telephone 0800 567123

The National Aids Trust
6th Floor
Eileen House
80 Newington Causeway
London
SE1 6EF

Telephone 071 972 2845

Terence Higgins Trust
52–54 Grays Inn Road
London
WC1X 8JU

Telephone 071 831 0330

DRUGS

Drug abuse is becoming of increasing concern to employers. The extent of drug abuse at all levels of the organisation appears to be escalating and the detrimental effect that this can have on employees' performance and behaviour is becoming recognised as a major problem.

Employers who fail to handle problems of drug abuse may be liable both under the Misuse of Drugs Act 1971 and under the Health and Safety at Work Act 1974.

The Misuse of Drugs Act divides controlled drugs into three classes according to their level of danger:

CLASS A

Includes cocaine, opioids (including heroin, morphine and opium), hallucinogenics and psychomimetics (including LSD, mescalin, PCP or "Angel Dust"), Class B drugs prepared for injection.

CLASS B

Includes amphetamines, barbiturates, cannabis, methaqualone (Mandrax).

CLASS C

Includes less harmful amphetamines, tranquillisers (such as Valium).

Certain medicinal preparations containing low concentrations of controlled drugs eg kaolin and morphine, codeine linctus, and a number of prescription-only tranquillisers have been exempted from the offence of unlawful possession.

The list of controlled drugs is being continually updated as new drugs are developed or become misused. Under the Misuse of Drugs Act 1971 it is an offence:

- to possess, supply, offer to supply or produce controlled drugs without authorisation.
  There is a defence against the charge if possession was taken to prevent someone from committing an offence and steps were taken to hand the drugs over to the police or to destroy them

- to allow them to be supplied or offered for supply or produced on the premises or to allow cannabis or opium to be smoked on the premises. It is not an offence to allow the use of other controlled drugs.

Where drugs are prepared and used on the employer's premises the employer could be liable under the above Act.

If an employer ignores the fact that employees are in possession or are supplying drugs in the workplace than the employer is at risk of committing an offence.

Under common law it is an offence to "aid and abet" the committing of an offence under the Misuse of Drugs Act.

EMPLOYERS' RESPONSIBILITIES

In addition to the common law duty implicit in every contract of employment to take reasonable care for the health and safety of its employees, the Health and Safety at Work Act 1974 now imposes a statutory duty of care on the employer "to ensure so far as is reasonably practicable, the health and safety of its employees". It is a criminal offence to be in breach of this duty.

This particularly includes the provision of safe systems of work and adequate supervision.

The Health and Safety at Work Act also reinforces common law in that employers are now under a statutory obligation to conduct their undertakings in such a way as to ensure that third parties eg contractors, suppliers, customers, and the public are not exposed to health and safety risks. A breach of this duty is a criminal offence.

As far as drug abuse is concerned the Health and Safety at Work Act places an obligation on the employer to ensure that its employees are not in a position where they can cause injury to themselves or others or cause damage in the workplace because of the effects of drugs. This means that if an employee is required to operate machinery or equipment or to drive, and is under the influence of drugs, if an accident occurs at work, the employer may be vicariously liable for the employee's actions.

EMPLOYEES' RESPONSIBILITIES

Again, under the Health and Safety at Work Act employees have a statutory duty to take reasonable care for the health and safety of themselves and their colleagues who may be affected by their acts or omissions at work. They can be sued for negligence if they fail to do so. Therefore, an employee would be in breach of this duty if he or she was under the influence of drugs and his or her judgement was impaired resulting in carelessness in work processes which could cause risk to himself or herself or colleagues.

Employees are also required to co-operate with their employer to enable the employer to comply with his or her own duties under the Act. This includes following rules and procedures which are laid down to ensure that safe working practices are adopted.

THE EFFECTS OF DRUG ABUSE ON THE EMPLOYER

Drug abuse may be causing an employer damage in a number of ways:

POOR ATTENDANCE

Employees who are misusing drugs will most likely take more sick leave than the average employee.

Timekeeping is likely to become erratic.

ACCIDENTS

Accidents may occur involving either the drug abuser or, because of his or her negligence, to others.

QUALITY AND QUANTITY OF WORK

The quality of work is likely to suffer with more mistakes being made, which in turn will mean that business could be lost through shoddy workmanship or extra time and money spent by others trying to put things right. This will lead to less work being achieved all round.

Bad decisions could be taken which might lead to costly or even dangerous mistakes occurring.

WORKING RELATIONSHIPS

Relationships with colleagues may become strained causing problems in a number of ways:

If the employee works in a team environment then co-operation and teamwork may suffer.

Relationships with those in authority may become impossible as the employee becomes more difficult to motivate and control.

If the employee is responsible for others, then respect and credibility will eventually be lost, making it difficult to effectively manage his or her own subordinates.

If the employee is involved with customers or clients then these relationships may become damaged resulting in a lost contract or sale. The reputation of the organisation may become tarnished, leading to more widespread loss of business.

CRIME

Increasing dependency upon drugs may mean that the drug abuser resorts to crime to fund an increasingly expensive habit. This may involve stealing money from colleagues or the organisation. It may involve stealing goods where these can be sold to third parties to raise cash or be exchanged for drugs.

REPUTATION

As stated above, the reputation of the employer may become tarnished in the eyes of prospective clients. Prospective new recruits may choose to look elsewhere rather than join an organisation which is well known for the wrong reasons!

RECOGNITION OF DRUG ABUSE

It is important, if there is a problem of drug abuse, that it is recognised as early as possible. This will help the employee concerned to have a greater chance of early rehabilitation and will increase the likelihood of his or her being able to make a full recovery and a return to normal, productive employment.

Since the majority of employers are not medical experts the way to recognise whether or not there is a problem is to monitor the performance of staff to identify whether there have been any significant changes in work patterns or levels of attendance.

Many organisations will have a formal system of staff appraisal whereby staff are assessed in terms of their overall performance on a regular basis. Staff appraisal interviews provide an opportunity for both employer and employee to set time aside so that both parties have the opportunity of discussing fully all aspects of an employee's work and whether any problems are being experienced.

Typically, a staff appraisal will cover such areas as the quality and quantity of work being achieved; whether the employee is experiencing any difficulties with any aspects of his or her work or working relationships; his or her aspirations and interests in terms of his or her own career direction and whether future training or coaching might be appropriate. It also provides an opportunity to discuss any other problems which may be affecting an employee's attitude to work as well as providing a formal framework for the line manager to show appreciation for work well done.

A well conducted staff appraisal may well lay the foundations for an employee who may not have felt able to disclose his or her habit to be able to do so in the knowledge that the meeting is intended to be constructive concerning his or her performance and future with the organisation, as well as being confidential.

In addition to staff appraisal interviews many employers operate a system of communication whereby employee and boss get together on a more informal "one to one" basis to discuss every day issues and problems. These meetings can provide an ideal opportunity for employers to detect whether there have been any changes in the employee's standard of performance which may be indicators that something is wrong.

A good system of monitoring attendance for all employees across the board will also highlight whether there have been any changes in attendance patterns that require further investigation.

The following may be indicators of an employee suffering from the effects of drug abuse:

- Sudden increases in days off work through sickness or for unauthorised absences

- Erratic timekeeping

- Sudden decrease in the amount of work undertaken

- Unexpectedly poor quality work

- Significant mistakes and misjudgements

- Missed deadlines

- Unexpected complaints from customers

- Deteriorating relationships with colleagues

- Untypical patterns of behaviour such as swearing or fighting

- Deterioration in personal hygiene

These indicators may also serve as early warning signals for a number of other problems and care should be taken not to jump to the wrong conclusions.

Employees who have personal problems for a variety of different reasons may well react in a similar way. For example, an employee may be suffering from problems with relationships either at home or at work, it may be that the work itself is unsuitable and manifesting itself in the employee's behaviour. Other problems at work such as bullying and harassment may lead to similar symptoms being experienced even though the problem is of a different nature.

Further material evidence of drug misuse that may come to light may include:

- scorched tinfoil, tinfoil tubes, matchbox covers

- syringes, needles, needle caps

- scorched spoons

- small mirror, razor, straws

- twists or squares of paper (for holding powder substances)

TACKLING THE PROBLEM

In the first instance it is suggested that an employee who is suffering from drug abuse should be treated in the same way as someone with a medical condition.

The intention should be to encourage the employee to seek professional help and treatment as soon as possible with a view to being fit and able to continue with his or her employment.

However, if the employee refuses to accept help or fails to continue with the necessary treatment, then future lapses in behaviour and performance should be dealt with through the normal Disciplinary Procedure.

As with other sensitive issues a company policy setting out how drug abuse will be tackled within the organisation will help to encourage employees who are drug abusers to come forward in the knowledge that the employer is willing to provide constructive help, instead of assuming that the issue will automatically be treated as a disciplinary issue.

A constructive policy will show employees and line management how such matters should be tackled and will confirm publicly the organisation's supportive attitude in dealing with it.

Typically, a policy will include:

- Drug abuse is a problem that may occur at any level in an organisation. The policy should therefore state that it applies to everyone regardless of status.

- A key feature of any policy is that such matters should remain confidential to encourage employees to come forward to seek help. Employees should be assured that the matter will be treated in strictest confidence and that it will only be disclosed to those that need to know with their prior permission.

- Although employees with a drug problem should be encouraged to seek help of their own free will they should be aware that to refuse to accept help may lead to disciplinary action being taken if they are unable to meet and maintain the standards of performance and conduct required of them.

- The employer will undertake to ensure that any employee with a drug problem will be offered advice, help and access to treatment if appropriate. The size of the organisation and the amount of resources, if any, that an employer feels able to make available to fund treatment will vary from organisation to organisation.

- The policy should spell out the employer's and the employees' duties towards ensuring a safe and healthy working environment for all employees and others so that the employee who is suffering from drug abuse is aware of the implications if the habit affects his or her standard of work performance and he or she does not seek help.

- Any absences for treatment and for rehabilitation should be treated in the same way as any other sickness absence.

- Wherever possible the employee should be able to return to the same job following treatment. Where this is not possible every attempt to provide an alternative should be made in the same way as for other employees with medical problems.

The employer will need to decide whether it will be possible to protect earnings or whether the employee will be offered the appropriate salary and benefits for the new position.

- If the employee refuses to accept help or refuses to continue with treatment and their performance or conduct continues to deteriorate then they will be treated in accordance with the disciplinary procedure which may lead to their dismissal.

- All employees will be provided with information and training so that:

— Employees are made aware that if they suffer from drug related problems then the employer will treat the matter sympathetically and that help will be provided to assist them in resolving their problem.

— Management and supervision will be made aware of the organisation's policy concerning drug abuse so that they know how to recognise a problem and how they should respond should an issue arise.

— Contacts will be established with suitable outside bodies who are able to offer professional advice and treatment so that employees are aware of who to contact and what they must do to seek help.

DISMISSALS

Dismissals related to drug misuse whether off or on-duty are potentially fair provided that they have been handled fairly and in line with appropriate procedures.

Such dismissals will be either on grounds of:

CAPABILITY

Where an employee is suffering from drug addiction they should be treated as any other employee would be treated with a medical condition. The fairness of the dismissal will therefore depend on the employer's establishing the true medical condition and giving the employee a reasonable period of time in which to recover.

or

CONDUCT

If an employee commits isolated acts related to drugs then provided the proper disciplinary procedures have been followed dismissal will be seen to be fair.

SCREENING FOR DRUGS

Testing for drugs is not that common in the workplace although some large employers including BP, British Rail, Esso and Texaco have introduced such policies.

The types of drugs that employers will normally screen for are barbiturates, canabis, cocaine, ecstasy, heroin and LSD by carrying out tests on urine samples. One of the difficulties with carrying out these tests is that they are not wholly accurate and if an individual knows that a test is due to be taken then he or she can avoid taking drugs beforehand so that they will not show up in the tests.

There are currently no legal guidelines concerning employers testing for drugs or concerning keeping the test results confidential. There is therefore nothing to stop the employer from notifying the police of any individuals whose test results are shown to be positive.

PRE-EMPLOYMENT DRUG SCREENING

Many organisations require their prospective employees to undergo a medical which may include drug screening as a pre-condition of employment. Those applicants who do not wish to be tested are therefore in a position where they may choose to withdraw their application for employment. In any event, as mentioned above, the results of the test will not necessarily be foolproof although where positive tests results do show up it will enable the employer to sift out those applicants who could otherwise create problems in the long term.

DRUG SCREENING FOR EXISTING EMPLOYEES

A drug test cannot be carried out on an employee without his or her prior consent otherwise it may be classified as an assault on the individual which could lead to civil or criminal charges being brought against the employer.

It may also be a breach of the implied term of trust and confidence to require an employee to undergo drug screening where the contract of employment does not include a provision for such testing. However, if there are special health and safety considerations, for example, if an employee is suspected of drug abuse or if he or she has been involved in an accident at work, then it may be seen as reasonable for the employer to require the tests to be undertaken.

If an employee does make a claim for breach of contract then he or she would have to show that there had been some financial loss involved. An alternative, assuming that the individual had accrued sufficient service, would be to make a claim of constructive dismissal at Industrial Tribunal. The Tribunal would then consider:

- Whether there had been any prior consultation with the employee

- The reasons for the introduction of drug screening eg health and safety risks, suspected drug abuse

- Whether an assurance was given that the results of the tests would be treated in confidence

- Whether the correct procedures were followed.

INTRODUCING A DRUG SCREENING POLICY

As with the introduction of any new policy of a sensitive nature, the following steps should be followed:

CONSULTATION

Employees and, where they exist, their staff representatives or shop stewards should be consulted and their agreement sought. The written consent of individual employees should also be obtained.

They should be provided with the reasons why the organisation is concerned to introduce such a policy. This may be because the nature of the work is such that there is a health and safety risk to employees, the organisation's clients or the general public if sufficient safeguards are not in place. A typical example of this may be a train driver or a tanker driver where the occurrence of an accident is more likely than with someone working at a desk.

The procedures should be made known so that employees know how the testing will be carried out and what will happen to the results.

FREQUENCY OF TESTING

The policy should state the frequency with which tests will be conducted and whether employees will be given prior warning of the tests. Many employers carry out tests without prior warning of the actual date so that employees cannot affect the results by not taking drugs beforehand.

Organisations such as Texaco test applicants as part of the selection procedure. Future tests on staff are carried out on a random basis. In particularly safety sensitive areas such as their oil refinery, employees will be tested on a monthly basis.

CONFIDENTIALITY

Unfortunately there are no legal guidelines concerning the confidentiality of the results of drug tests undertaken by or on behalf of the employer, which means that employees may be concerned that the police may be informed which could result in their conviction under the Misuse of Drugs Act.

To gain the co-operation of staff the policy should therefore give an undertaking that disclosure will only be made with the consent of the employee concerned and in the interests of providing help and support in tackling the problem.

Employees who are under prescribed medication should be asked to inform their employer of this, in confidence, prior to tests being carried out so that this may be taken into account when assessing the test results.

PROVISION OF HELP

It should be made clear in the policy that the employer will be sympathetic to those employees who show a positive test result and that help will be provided.

APPEALS

The policy should include provision for employees to appeal so that they can put forward any mitigating circumstances or seek a check on the results if they are concerned about the accuracy of the test.

If appropriate, the employee should be given the opportunity of producing a letter from his or her doctor to support his or her explanations.

The arrangements for appealing should be made clear: for example, who they should contact, whether it should be in writing and the timescale for making the appeal.

WHAT TO DO ABOUT EMPLOYEES WHO REFUSE TO SUBMIT TO TESTING

If screening for drugs is included in the contract of employment and an employee refuses to comply, then the employer may be left with no alternative but to take the employee through the disciplinary procedure.

Unfortunately, if an exception is made which allows the employee to opt out then a precedent will be set allowing future employees to expect similar exceptions to be permitted.

However, care should be taken not to ruin an otherwise satisfactory employment relationship particularly where there are no grounds to suspect that there is a problem of drug abuse.

USEFUL ADDRESSES

Turning Point
9–12 Long Lane
London
EC1A 9HA
Telephone No. 071 606 3947

Re-Solv
St Mary's Chambers
19 Station Road
Stone
Staffordshire
ST15 8JP

TRANSVESTITES AND TRANSEXUALS

RECOGNISING TRANSVESTISM AND TRANSEXUALISM

Although it is not very common, it is helpful to have established certain principles on how one would handle such a situation if it did occur in the workplace. It is always much easier to consider principles and develop a policy when there are no emotive pressures demanding hasty decisions.

Transvestism, or "gender dysphoria" which is the medical condition commonly known as transvestism, is a compulsion to wear the clothing of the opposite sex without actually wanting to change sex. Although transvestites are of both sexes the majority of them are men. In recent research it has been found that one in every 1,000 males is a transvestite.

Most transvestites take great care not to be "found out" even by their spouses because of the fear and guilt of their compulsion. This means that very few transvestites are known to want to live full-time in the opposite gender and because of this they are unlikely to want to "cross-dress" in the working environment.

Whereas transvestism tends to be covert, transexualism is different in that the individual usually wishes to live in the opposite gender and therefore the situation inevitably becomes public knowledge.

To be accepted for a sex-change operation, individuals have to be referred to a Gender Identity Clinic where they will go through stringent counselling before they are accepted for surgery. They are required to have lived and worked successfully as a member of the opposite sex for a year before the operation is undertaken. This will inevitably create a number of problems for an organisation, not least of which is which toilets the transexual should use!

It can take several years for a transexual to be accepted for surgery and subsequently go through the complete sex-change process so if the employee does want to remain with the same employer the implications for all concerned will need to be thought through very carefully.

LEGAL IMPLICATIONS

There is currently no British law which protects transvestites, transexuals, gays or lesbians from discrimination.

For example, in Ryder-Barratt v Alpha Training Limited, Mr Ryder-Barratt claimed that he had been discriminated against because he had been dismissed for wearing a skirt. The Tribunal dismissed the case on the grounds that the Sex Discrimination Act is intended to deal with discrimination on the grounds of a person's biological gender and does not extend to transexuality.

However an employee could claim unfair dismissal or constructive dismissal on the grounds that his or her conduct outside of the workplace is of no concern to the employer provided that such conduct does not have an adverse effect on the employer's business.

If the attitude of colleagues and/or the company's clients was such that the employer's business could be put in severe difficulty and the situation was irretrievable, then dismissal may be justifiable.

PROBLEMS THAT MAY OCCUR

Many transexuals try to make a fresh start with a new job and new employer after their sex change operation where there is no need for their colleagues, other than a limited few who should treat the matter confidentially, to know about their circumstances.

However, because of the current economic climate it is possible that the employee may wish to remain with the employer and face the inevitable embarrassment and problems that will undoubtedly occur.

CHANGING NAMES AND APPEARANCE

An existing employee who is a transexual will probably wish to be reclassified at work and dress as a member of the opposite sex. Although birth certificates cannot be changed, names can be changed by deed poll and other official documents amended accordingly.

There is no reason why companies cannot reclassify the employee as far as their records are concerned and an obvious time to do this would be on return from the sex-change operation if it is the employee's intention to undergo surgery.

CROSS-DRESSING

As mentioned above, in most cases, transvestites keep their compulsion a secret and therefore their wish to cross-dress in the workplace is unlikely to occur. However, it is unlikely that it would be seen as reasonable for a transvestite to insist on "cross-dressing" at work although if they registered with the Gender Identity Clinic then they could be regarded as pre-operative transexuals.

ADVICE TO COLLEAGUES

Both management and other colleagues will be better able to cope with the situation if they are consulted and advised on the nature of the conditions and the stress and anxiety that this can cause transvestites/transexuals. Again, with the agreement of the employees concerned, guidance can be given to work colleagues to provide understanding to help with acceptance and integration of the transvestites/transexuals at work.

CASE STUDY

When George applied for a job with a computer software house as a systems analyst he stated in his letter of application that he was a transexual and in the process of undergoing a gender change. George was invited to attend an interview during which they discussed not only his suitability to do the job in terms of his skills and abilities but also the potential problems of employing a transexual.

It was agreed with George that the company would talk to their female employees to see if there were any objections in employing him. Only a minority said they were unsure and George was subsequently taken on. Georgina, as she became known, was soon accepted by her colleagues and was respected as an individual in her own right.

Some larger organisations use the services of an outside counsellor to provide information and/or briefings to employees, although if resources are limited this may be achieved through the usual informal briefings or departmental meetings that would normally take place as part of day to day communication between management and employees.

Colleagues should also be told what particular arrangements will apply both pre-operative and post-operative where this is applicable. For example, what the person is to be called or addressed as both in correspondence and in introductions to clients.

One of the more difficult problems to resolve is where an employee is living and working in the opposite gender but has not had the sex-change operation and is cross-dressed. There are likely to be objections and even harassment from the men if there is a "man" dressed in a skirt using the men's facilities and equally there are likely to be objections from the women if a "man" is using the women's toilets, washing or changing facilities.

Employees should be advised of the arrangements that will apply concerning the use of facilities.

TOILETS, WASHING AND CHANGING FACILITIES

Before the sex-change operation takes place, the ideal answer is to designate unisex facilities as for disabled people although this may not be possible in a small company with limited facilities and there is no legal requirement for an employer to provide separate facilities under these circumstances.

After the change has taken place the employee should be recognised and accepted as a man or a woman and be able to use the appropriate facilities for a man or woman although there may well be initial apprehension.

ATTITUDES

Problems are unlikely to be limited to the toilets and the employer will need to be prepared to provide guidelines and advice to management and employees to ensure that a transexual is treated as fairly and sympathetically as any other employee, particularly during the transition stage. For example, any instances of bullying or harassment should be dealt with as for any other employee.

The attitude of senior management towards a transvestite or transexual will strongly influence the way in which the individual will be able to successfully continue in the workplace. If there is open understanding and continued confidence in the employee to continue satisfactorily with his or her career then future acceptance and integration in the workplace is more likely to be achieved. Often though it is the employee who cannot face remaining with the employer and who may choose to make a fresh start elsewhere where he or she is not known and his or her past can be revealed in confidence only to those that need to know.

TARGETS FOR BLACKMAIL

As stated above, transvestites usually wish to keep their compulsion a secret which means that those who are engaged in highly sensitive or confidential areas could be ideal targets for blackmail if the knowledge got into the wrong hands. Similarly, employees in homosexual relations may be vulnerable to blackmail.

This could be a fair reason for dismissal for "some other substantial reason" if the employer was justified in his or her concerns about the effect that this could have on his or her business, and provided that consideration had first been given to transferring the employee to alternative work of a less sensitive or confidential nature.

Transexuals, unlike transvestites, want to "come out" and live as the opposite gender and therefore because there is no secret there is unlikely to be scope for blackmail.

AIDS

One of the fears of employing transvestites or transexuals is that they are seen as homosexual which leads to a fear of AIDS. Such fears can be allayed by educating those involved, both in terms of the AIDS virus and explaining about transvestites and transexuals.

WHAT THE EMPLOYER CAN DO TO HELP

TALK TO THE TRANSVESTITE/TRANSEXUAL

Discuss the matter openly but in confidence with the employee concerned so that you understand what the employee is trying to achieve and how he or she wishes to see his or her future. Agree with the employee what support you are able to give and how you propose to go about it.

ADVICE TO MANAGEMENT

With the prior agreement of the transvestite/transexual, advise management involved with the employee how to handle matters officially within the organisation eg calling the employee by his or her chosen name; amending employee records.

Management should be instructed that transvestites and transexuals should be treated no less favourably than any other employees when handling promotions, transfers, opportunities for further training etc.

Management should be encouraged to be understanding and give support and show continued confidence in the employee: this will substantially affect how others behave towards him or her.

ADVICE TO COLLEAGUES

Both management and other colleagues will be better able to cope with the problem if they are consulted and advised on the nature of the conditions of transvestism and transexualism and the stress and anxiety that this can cause those affected by it.

Again, with the agreement of the transvestites/ transexuals concerned, guidance can be given to employees to provide understanding to help with their acceptance and integration at work.

Employees should be advised of the arrangements that will apply concerning use of facilities both pre-operative and post-operative where this is applicable.

As mentioned above, there is the commonly held view that transvestites and transexuals are usually homosexual with the inevitable assumption that there is a risk of AIDS. Dealing with AIDS is described separately in this book.

FURTHER INFORMATION

Further advice can be obtained from LAGER (Lesbian and Gay Employment Rights) at St Margaret's House, 21 Old Ford Road, Bethnal Green, London E2 9PL. Telephone 081 983 0694.

ALCOHOL

Until recently drinking at work, before work or during working hours was accepted as being nothing out of the ordinary. It used to be commonplace for canteens and staff restaurants to provide beer or wines as part of the service or for the Social Club to be open for the sale of alcohol during work breaks.

When entertaining customers and clients it was the "done thing" to go out to lunch either at a local restaurant or to the organisation's executive dining room and be plied with aperitifs before the meal and wine on tap during the meal.

When recruiting prospective new employees at senior level, they may be taken out for lunch to meet other members of the team on a more informal basis: again it would have seemed odd in the past if alcoholic drinks had not been provided.

Is it any wonder that alcohol-related problems are on the increase, particularly in occupations that involve a lot of entertainment with business contacts and clients?

In recent years there has been an about-turn with many organisations withdrawing alcohol altogether from the menu for employees at all levels of the organisation, from the shop floor to senior director level as it becomes more apparent that alcohol and work do not mix.

The cost of alcohol misuse is said by the Department of Employment to run into hundreds of millions of pounds each year and it is inevitable that each organisation is likely to have at least someone who is affected by alcoholism.

EFFECTS OF ALCOHOLISM ON THE EMPLOYER

Employees whose performance at work is impaired by the use of alcohol will affect the employer in many ways, for example:

SICKNESS

Sickness levels will increase and although the reasons given will probably be headaches, stomach upsets etc it is more than likely that the true cause could be hangovers.

In a recent Industrial Society survey, the cost of sickness absence overall was estimated at costing industry around £9 billion as a result of around 200 million working days being lost each year.

ATTENDANCE

Time-keeping is likely to become more erratic both from the point of view of lateness as employees find it more difficult to get out of bed in the mornings as well as prolonged lunch breaks spent at the pub or in the local wine bar.

EFFECT ON WORKING RELATIONSHIPS

Employees who have to cover for colleagues who are either not there through lateness or because they are unwell due to alcohol will become resentful.

Employees who are responsible for others will lose the respect of their subordinates. Their credibility and ability to manage effectively will eventually become undermined by their subordinates' attitudes towards them.

ACCIDENTS

Accidents are much more likely to occur when individuals are under the influence of alcohol. Judgement may become impaired, skylarking may occur and tempers may flare resulting in avoidable accidents occurring either to the individual or to other employees.

LOSS OF PRODUCTION

Production losses could be high resulting from fewer hours worked through sickness or accidents.

Equipment and materials may become damaged through carelessness.

Goods or other services may be rejected because they do not meet quality standards.

LOST BUSINESS OPPORTUNITIES

Opportunities could be lost by those responsible for negotiating business deals. Future potentially lucrative contacts could be destroyed when attempting to establish a business relationship if judgement is impaired and the situation misread.

Deals that are made may be disastrous to the organisation if negotiated through a haze of magnanimity, or alternatively they may be lost altogether as respect and credibility are destroyed in the eyes of the other party.

WHY PEOPLE TURN TO DRINK

There are many reasons why a build up of stress and anxiety may lead people to turn to drink. There may be problems at work, in which case the employer could well be in a position to help with resolving the problem. For example:

VOLUME OF WORK

If people have too much or even too little work, then this may affect them. If someone is overloaded then the worry and anxiety of being able to cope may be eased by turning to drink or he or she may feel that a drink will help him or her to keep going for longer stretches at a time by giving that extra lift.

Equally a person who is under-utilised is just as likely to become bored and frustrated with the lack of challenge and interest.

When planning work loads it is important that employers are realistic in their expectations of their employees and that channels of communication are set up so that employees who do have concerns with their work will be listened to and where appropriate remedial action can be taken.

BORING WORK

Boring or monotonous work for some people may be difficult to cope with for prolonged periods at a time, and may end up driving them up the wall!

An easy solution for them may be to have a drink to break the monotony and cheer themselves up.

As above, part of management's role is to plan work that is as rewarding and interesting as possible so that their employees feel fulfilled and happy at their jobs.

UNSOCIAL HOURS

Employees who work long or irregular hours will often feel the need for a drink to help them cope with their pattern of work.

It may be that a re-examination of the working arrangements or task planning may enable more acceptable hours to be worked, or, where this is not possible, the provision of suitable work breaks with non-alcoholic refreshments may help to ease the strain.

OVER PROMOTION

Often, employees are over-promoted or employees who are particularly good in their existing roles are promoted to managerial positions for which they are really not suited. This may well lead to extra worry and stress especially for employees who have been used to being good, high performers and then find that they are unable to cope with the new demands made of them.

Care should be taken by employers in selecting staff to fill any position that they first carefully identify all the requirements of the job. This will include skill requirements as well as the personal requirements of the job.

This will enable them to select suitable candidates by matching their work skills, abilities and personal attributes to the actual job to be filled rather than assume that someone who has been good in one job can automatically be as effective in another job even though it requires totally different abilities.

A typical example of this is the top salesman who has a high level of selling skills and product knowledge but is not so hot on paperwork being promoted to Sales Manager. Here the key requirements are budgeting, forecasting, work delegation etc, which do not require his/her sales skills but need a high degree of administrative ability.

OCCUPATIONS WITH ACCESS TO ALCOHOL

There are many jobs which provide ready access to alcohol.

For example restaurant, hotel and bar staff will continually be working in an environment where drinks are readily accessible, generally flowing, and they may be regularly pressurised into having a drink by the customers themselves.

Many sales people and senior management are in positions where they are in constant contact with clients and customers and are expected to wine and dine them as part of their normal routine activities.

Breweries have until recently supplied their products freely to their employees during the normal course of the working day. People who work for importers of wines and other alcoholic beverages may well have much freer access to alcohol as part of their working lives.

Organisations will need to consider carefully what their policy is to be regarding drinking whilst on duty and how they tackle excessive drinking as well as alcoholism.

WORKING ALONE

There are a number of occupations where people work alone all the time, often without any supervision. For example security guards, drivers, assistants in some small off licences or shops. The temptation to have a drink to keep them company can become a habit on which they become increasingly dependent.

The organisation's rules and policies should be made clear to employees so that they understand the implications of their actions and that a choice may need to be made if they wish to stay in their jobs.

WORKING RELATIONSHIPS

There may be problems with work colleagues which may result from a variety of causes. For example, there may be personality clashes between colleagues or with management; there may even be problems with sexual or racial harassment or bullying generally.

There may be pressure from peer colleagues or even the boss to imbibe!

If good communication systems are set up it will help to identify early on any potential problems that could eventually lead to matters causing undue stress and anxiety which could lead to the individual turning to drink for moral support.

For example, regular "one-to-one" meetings with employees to discuss work related matters as well as staff appraisals on a more formal but regular basis will help to establish a framework whereby employees and management are able to discuss matters in a confidential environment in the knowledge that they will be listened to and supported.

In the past employees were encouraged to leave their personal problems at home.

Organisations are now realising that by assisting their employees to overcome their personal problems, employees are more likely to return to productive working quickly.

It is fast becoming recognised that a healthy, happy employee is of more value to the organisation than one who is overcome and sinking fast with problems which may in turn lead him or her to seek solace in alcohol.

Typically personal or social problems may include:

MARITAL OR FAMILY PROBLEMS

While the employer may not wish to get involved with the detail of the problem, it may be that help can be provided in a number of ways.

It may be possible to allow time off to be given to enable the employee to attend to matters rather than be forced to "telephone in sick". Rather than lose pay it may be possible to make arrangements for the employee either to re-organise his or her work times for a short period or take time off without pay or from holiday entitlement.

Depending on the size of the organisation and resources, counsellors will often be available to give support and advice on a range of issues or alternatively they may be able to refer employees on to established contacts who specialise in dealing with such problems.

ILLNESS WITHIN THE FAMILY

As above, a problem shared is often a problem halved. Depending upon the extent of the problem, it may be possible to allow the employee to re-organise his or her working commitments or to take work home or take additional leave, either with or without pay. This would enable him or her to attend to his or her family without the additional fear of losing his or her job through poor attendance.

BEREAVEMENT

If an organisation has an established policy on how their managers should treat employees who have suffered bereavement after they return to work, this may help the person concerned come to terms more quickly with his or her loss.

As above, depending on the size of organisation and resources, counsellors may be employed to help employees through these difficult times or alternatively they may have contacts where help can be provided.

If the employer is supportive instead of pushing the matter under the carpet, the employee will recover much more quickly and be less likely to sink into the depths of despair and a bottle.

FINANCIAL PROBLEMS

Often financial problems will lead an individual to drink to try to ease the worry of how he or she is going to cope. The cost of the drinking is likely to result in even greater debt in view of the expense of sustaining the habit.

A sympathetic ear from the employer may help the employee to break the cycle by talking through his or her problems and perhaps encouraging him or her to seek professional advice from a qualified financial adviser.

SOCIAL HABIT

Often an individual's social life may be geared to drinking either at home or in the pub. There may be social pressures to drink vast quantities in order to be socially acceptable within his or her social group!

The organisation's rules and procedures will help to make the employee realise that perhaps a choice has to be made between having a good time and holding down a job.

As mentioned above, a number of organisations now train some of their employees to act as counsellors. They may be attached to the Medical Department, the Personnel Department or even selected from the work force generally and are trained to provide advice and guidance to employees on a range of personal problems.

In addition to this contacts may be established with outside organisations so that employees can be referred, with their agreement, to seek further help. Such help may sometimes be funded by the organisation and will be seen as a good investment towards getting their employees back to fruitful employment as quickly as possible.

Some organisations pay a subscription to organisations providing a range of counselling services on behalf of their employees so that they are able to seek confidential advice, without the need for the employer to even know, on a wide range of personal issues ranging from marital or bereavement counselling to providing financial advice to those who have got themselves into money difficulties.

EMPLOYERS' RESPONSIBILITIES

As stated elsewhere in this book, employers have both a common law duty of care under the contract of employment as well as a statutory personal duty of care under the Health and Safety at Work Act 1974 "to ensure so far as is reasonably practicable, the health and safety of its employees". It is a criminal offence to be in breach of this duty.

EMPLOYEES' RESPONSIBILITIES

Employees also have a statutory duty under the Health and Safety at Work Act 1974 to take reasonable care for the health and safety of themselves and their colleagues who may be affected by their acts or omissions at work. If employees fail to take reasonable care and an accident occurs, they can be sued for negligence.

Therefore if an employee under the influence of drink, whose judgement was impaired as a result of this, caused an accident injuring either himself or herself or a colleague as a result of his or her carelessness or negligence, he or she could be sued for damages.

RECOGNITION OF AN ALCOHOL PROBLEM

Many organisations will already have a formal system of monitoring employees' performance either through regular "one-to-one" meetings between management and subordinates or through the formal staff appraisal process.

Regular "one-to-one" meetings will provide an opportunity to meet frequently to review progress on a day to day or week to week basis and to discuss short-

term objectives, achievements, problems etc as they
occur. Although such meetings may well be fairly short,
depending upon the nature of the work and the seniority
of the employee, it should provide the opportunity for
a good working relationship to be established so that
problems can be aired and resolved before developing into
major issues which become insoluble.

Staff appraisals provide an ideal opportunity for both
parties to set a block of time aside, generally on an annual
basis, to discuss formally all aspects of the work and
whether any problems are being experienced. However,
it is important not to leave problems until the annual
appraisal but to deal with them at the time.

Staff appraisals will normally cover such issues as the
quality and quantity of work being achieved; whether the
employee is experiencing any difficulties with any aspects
of his or her work or working relationships; his or her
aspirations and interests in terms of his or her own career
and whether future training might be appropriate; it also
provides an opportunity to discuss any other problems
which may be affecting an employee's attitude to work as
well as providing a formal framework for the line manager
to give praise for work well done.

If the staff appraisal is well conducted then it will
provide the ideal opportunity for employees to be able to
open up and discuss matters of concern to them with their
line manager in an atmosphere which is confidential and
constructive.

Monitoring attendance and time-keeping for all
employees will help to highlight whether there have been
any changes in attendance patterns which may give an
indication that all is not well and that further investigation
is required.

The following symptoms may give an indication
that an employee is suffering from the effects of alcohol

misuse. It should however be remembered that they could also be as a result of other problems eg drug abuse, or any number of other personal problems which are giving the employee cause for concern.

- An increase in latenesses and days off sick
- A deterioration in the quality and quantity of work
- Unreliability
- Poor relationships with colleagues
- Impaired concentration, memory and judgement
- Accidents

TACKLING THE PROBLEM

ALCOHOL MISUSE AS A MEDICAL CONDITION

In the first instance it is suggested that an employee who is misusing alcohol be treated in the same way as someone with a medical condition.

Employees should be encouraged to seek professional help and treatment as soon as possible with a view to their being fit and able to continue with their employment.

If an employee refuses to accept help or fails to continue with the necessary treatment then future lapses in behaviour or standards of performance should be dealt with through the normal Disciplinary Procedure.

As with other sensitive issues such as Drug or Substance Abuse a company policy should be established setting out how alcohol problems will be dealt with in the organisation. This will encourage employees to seek help voluntarily in the knowledge that their employer is willing to provide constructive help instead of assuming that the issue will be automatically treated as a disciplinary issue.

A constructive policy will show employees and line management how such matters should be tackled and will confirm publicly the organisation's supportive attitude towards dealing with it.

ALCOHOL MISUSE AS A CONDUCT ISSUE

In many instances, the misuse of alcohol by an employee is not medically related but down to the employee simply drinking when it is banned or drinking too much. How seriously such lapses in behaviour will be treated will depend on the organisation's own policy towards alcohol and its effect on work. The organisation's rules and procedures should make it clear to all employees if drinking is banned altogether or, if it is not, what will happen to employees whose behaviour or standards of performance are affected by alcohol.

However, as above, lapses in behaviour or standards of performance should be dealt with through the normal Disciplinary Procedure.

CASE STUDY

Roger worked in the chemical laboratory of a film processing plant. His duties involved mixing and testing large quantities of chemicals prior to their use in the mass developing of film. In view of the potential risks to both his own safety and that of his colleagues, and the potentially irretrievable damage that could be done to the film, being under the influence of drink at the workplace was viewed as a matter of serious misconduct.

Case Study (continued)

Roger had developed the habit of going for a drink most Friday lunchtimes and on several occasions had returned to work both late and extremely merry. His manager had cautioned him on a number of these occasions, pointing out the risks that he was causing and that being under the influence of drink was considered to be a serious misdemeanour which could result in a summary dismissal.

Unfortunately Roger disregarded these cautions and returned from lunch one Friday clearly under the influence of drink. Following a disciplinary hearing Roger was dismissed summarily for gross misconduct.

CASE STUDY

By contrast, Joe had been employed in the Post Room for a number of years and had been promoted to Post Room Supervisor several years ago. His work had always been to a high standard and he was well liked by both his subordinates and his "customers".

It became increasingly apparent that he spent an excessive amount of time in the pub across the road from his office and that his attendance was becoming more and more erratic. Overall, the number of hours he worked were well in excess of those required of him but he was frequently not around when urgent jobs needed to be organised.

Informal meetings were held to discuss with him his irregular pattern of attendance and eventually he accepted that his drinking was affecting his health

Case Study (continued)

and his ability to meet the requirements of his job. Arrangements were made, with his commitment, to attend a special alcohol clinic to help him overcome his problem.

Initially everything went well. Joe attended the clinic regularly and was soon able to resume his duties with the full support of his colleagues and his manager. Unfortunately, after a while Joe starting drinking again and his attendance record deteriorated once more. Again he was encouraged to accept help and was formally warned that if he was unable to meet the standards required of his job then he would be subject to further disciplinary action which could eventually lead to dismissal.

Unfortunately for Joe, despite the support of his company in encouraging him to seek help and allowing him time off for medical assistance he was unable to continue with his treatment and he resumed his excessive drinking. He was eventually dismissed following a series of warnings for continuing to fail to meet the company's standards of performance.

DRAFTING AN ALCOHOL POLICY

Typically, a policy for dealing with alcohol misuse will include the following:

- The policy should apply to everyone in the organisation regardless of status.

    It will hardly be fair and consistent to ban beer from the canteen if aperitifs and wines continue to be served in the executive dining room.

- Employees should be assured that the matter will remain confidential so that they are encouraged to seek help voluntarily.

  Disclosure should only be made to those that need to know and with the employee's prior permission.

- Employees should be made aware that if they do have an alcohol problem and they refuse to accept help or they do not continue with their treatment disciplinary action may be taken against them if they are unable to meet and maintain the standards of performance and conduct required of them.

  If it is established that an employee's use or misuse of alcohol is not a medical problem but a matter of conduct then lapses in the standards of conduct or performance required of him or her will be dealt with through the Disciplinary Procedure.

- The employer will undertake to ensure that any employee with an alcohol problem will be offered advice, help and access to treatment if appropriate.

  The size of the organisation and the amount of resources, if any, that an employer may consider able to make available to fund treatment will vary from organisation to organisation.

- The policy should spell out the employer's and employees' duties towards ensuring a safe and healthy working environment for all employees and others who may be at the place of work so that the employee concerned is aware of the implications if his or her drinking affects his or her standard of work performance.

- Any absences for treatment and for rehabilitation should be treated in the same way as any other sickness absence.

- Whenever possible employees should be able to return to the same job following treatment. Where this is not possible every attempt to provide an alternative should be made in the same way as for other employees with medical problems.

  The employer will need to decide whether it will be possible to protect earnings or whether the employee will be offered the appropriate salary and benefits for the new position.

- If the employee refuses to accept help or refuses to continue with treatment and his or her performance or conduct continues to give cause for concern then he or she will be treated in accordance with the Disciplinary Procedure which could lead to dismissal.

- All employees will be provided with information and training so that
  - they are aware that if they suffer from alcohol related problems then the employer will treat the matter sympathetically and that help will be provided to assist them in resolving their problem.
  - Managers and supervisors will be made aware of the organisation's policy concerning alcohol misuse so that they know how to recognise a problem and how they should respond should an issue arise.

- Contacts will be established with suitable outside bodies who are able to offer professional advice and treatment so that employees are aware of who to contact and what they must do to seek help.

DISMISSALS

Dismissals related to drinking whether off or on duty are potentially fair, provided that they have been handled fairly and in line with appropriate procedures.

Such dismissals will be either on grounds of:

CAPABILITY

Where an employee is suffering from chronic alcoholism he or she should be treated as any other employee would be treated with a medical condition. The fairness of the dismissal will therefore depend on the employer's establishing the true medical condition and giving the employee a reasonable period of time in which to recover.

CONDUCT

If an employee commits isolated acts related to drink or breaches a company rule by being under the influence of drink at work then provided the proper disciplinary procedures have been followed dismissal will be seen to be fair.

USEFUL ADDRESSES

Alcoholics Anonymous
PO Box 1
Stonebow House
Stone Bow
York
YO1 2NJ

Telephone 0904 644026

Alcohol Concern
275 Gray's Inn Road
London
WC1X 8QF

Telephone 071 833 3471

SMOKING

Attitudes towards smoking have changed dramatically in recent years and there has been increasing pressure from non-smokers to be able to work in smoke-free environments.

Not so many years ago it was the non-smoker who complained about working in a smoky atmosphere who was considered to be the nuisance whereas now the opposite is generally the case!

More and more organisations are moving towards introducing no-smoking policies in the workplace, and this chapter looks at the legal implications of introducing such a policy both from the health and safety aspect and the contractual aspect as well as the practical issues involved.

LEGISLATION

HEALTH AND SAFETY LEGISLATION

Employers have a duty 'as far as is reasonably practicable' to ensure the health, safety and welfare of their employees (Section 2 of the Health and Safety at Work Act 1974). This means that employers who continue to ignore the potential effect that passive smoking may have on their employees could be in breach of both their statutory duty and common law duty of care.

Employees have a duty to take reasonable care at work for the safety of themselves and others (Section 7 of the above Act). Therefore, an employee who refuses to comply with a smoking policy or continues to smoke could be in breach of this duty.

The above duties are enforceable by criminal prosecution and an employer may be subjected to improvement or enforcement notices being issued by the Health and Safety Inspectorate.

CASE STUDY

A Ms Clay recently submitted a claim to the Social Security Commissioner for disablement benefit on the basis that she had suffered injury to her lungs as a result of inhaling tobacco smoke at work, and was successful.

However, although this was not a claim for damages against her employer under the provisions of the Health and Safety at Work Act, the implications of the Commissioner's findings, that Ms Clay suffered an accident and resultant personal injury on specific occasions as a result of inhaling tobacco smoke, may have far-reaching consequences for employers.

As yet there is no case law established under the Health and Safety at Work Act in respect of the effects of smoking, passive or otherwise, in the workplace. However, ASH (Action on Smoking and Health) have obtained a legal opinion which indicates that non-smokers who suffer from passive smoking in the workplace may be able to sue their employers for damage to their health.

IMPLICATIONS OF EC LAW

Following the EC Framework Directive, under the Management of Health and Safety at Work Regulations 1992, employers are now required to assess all risks in the workplace, implement necessary safety measures and communicate safety issues to all employees. Under the Workplace (Health, Safety and Welfare) Regulations 1992, employers are now required to provide separate rest facilities for smokers and non-smokers or to prohibit smoking in rest areas and rest rooms.

Failure to comply with the regulations may result in criminal proceedings being taken against both the employer and the employee who is responsible for ensuring compliance.

THE LAW OF NEGLIGENCE

It has now been established in UK law that a claim for negligence may be successful if an employer has failed to respond to the harmful effects of smoking in the workplace ie:

- If the employer can reasonably foresee that an employee, or other person, might suffer harm as a consequence of smoking

- If the risk was a probable one

- If the employer failed to take reasonable steps to guard against it

- If the employee did suffer harm as a consequence of the smoking

An employer may also be vicariously liable for loss and damage caused by employees' smoking regardless of whether or not smoking was forbidden, where the smoking was 'in the course of employment'. If a non-smoking policy exists it is therefore essential to ensure that it is enforced.

COMMON LAW DUTY OF CARE

An implied term in every contract of employment is the employer's duty of care to provide a safe place of work. Therefore if an employer becomes aware of any particular risk to any particular employee then they have a duty to respond to that risk by taking all reasonable steps to eliminate or minimise the risk. A failure to respond could give rise to a claim for unfair dismissal for breach of contract.

The legal opinion obtained by ASH concludes that employers are sufficiently aware of the dangers of passive smoking so that an employee who could establish the causal connection between injury and exposure to tobacco smoke at work could successfully sue his or her employer for damages.

THE RIGHT TO SMOKE AT WORK?

Employees do not have 'contractual right to smoke' at work where there is no ban or limitation on smoking established. Furthermore, it is lawful for an employer to advertise for and recruit only non-smokers and to incorporate a term in the contract of employment limiting or totally banning smoking at the workplace.

However, where there is no existing policy preventing employees from smoking at work, if the employer intends to introduce and enforce a no-smoking policy then the new rules will become a part of the contract of employment and enforcement will be controlled through the application of the disciplinary procedure in the same way as for other failures to meet standards of performance or conduct such as poor workmanship or poor timekeeping.

If the employer wishes to incorporate a new policy into the contract of employment then, as with any new or revised term, agreement must be sought from the employees. Agreement should ideally be in writing although it may be assumed that the employee has agreed if after the passage of time no objection has been raised.

CASE STUDY

In Dryden v Greater Glasgow Health Board (EAT Scotland) Ms Dryden's claim that she was constructively dismissed when her employer introduced a non-smoking policy failed.

Ms Dryden had been employed by the Health Board as a nursing auxiliary for 14 years and smoked around 30 cigarettes a day. Until 1991 the Health Board had provided areas in the workplace where employees were allowed to smoke but following the circulation of a consultative document it was decided to ban smoking totally. Letters were issued to employees giving notice of the change and offering advice and counselling to smokers. Ms Dryden resigned a few days after the policy was implemented and claimed constructive dismissal on the basis that the introduction of the no-smoking policy constituted a material breach of an implied contractual term.

EAT confirmed the Industrial Tribunal's view that there was no specific implied term in Ms Dryden's contract of employment to the effect that she would be entitled to have access to facilities for smoking during working hours. There was no basis for holding that there was any implied term that smoking would continue to be permitted either generally or in the case of Ms Dryden.

> **Case Study** (continued)
>
> It was found that an employer is entitled to make rules for the conduct of employees in the workplace within the scope of the contract. In Ms Dryden's case once it was established that there was no implied term entitling her to smoking facilities the rule introduced by her employer against smoking was seen to be lawful.

BENEFITS OF INTRODUCING A NO-SMOKING POLICY

In addition to the Health and Safety implications described above, there are many other reasons why more and more employers are moving towards employing non-smokers. The benefits of employing non-smokers include:

- higher levels of productivity
- less sickness absence
- reduced ventilation and air-conditioning costs
- reduced cleaning bills
- reduced risk of fire

INTRODUCING A NO-SMOKING POLICY

FORM A WORKING PARTY

It is a good idea to form a working party so that all members of the workforce are represented. Ideally the working party will include:

- A member of senior management

- A member of Personnel

- A member of the Occupational Health Department

- A member of the Health and Safety Committee

- A representative of the Trade Union

- A representative of the Staff Association

and there should be a balance of smokers and non-smokers including, if possible, ex-smokers to ensure that the group is not biased.

The terms of reference of the working party should be agreed from the outset. These may include:

- the target date for implementation

- reaching agreement on restricted areas and/or times when smoking is to be permitted

- deciding how any budget for providing help for people wishing to give up smoking should be spent

- deciding what to do about offenders eg discipline

- when the working party will be disbanded eg on implementation of the policy or whether it will retain a role following implementation

As with any committee roles should be identified, eg, Chairperson, note-taker, who is to be responsible for communicating to both staff and management. The arrangements for the meetings, eg, frequency, length of meetings, location if appropriate, should be planned at the outset so that both individuals and their line management know in advance what commitment they must be prepared to make.

RAISING AWARENESS

Before any action is formally taken to either survey staff on their views or to set dates for implementation it is worth raising the awareness of staff to the health hazards of smoking and passive smoking. Good use can be made of house journals or posters in the workplace so that employers get used to the idea that a no-smoking policy will be of benefit to all. The introduction of a policy at a later stage will then come as less of a culture shock and with a greater understanding of the reasons behind it.

CONSULT WITH ALL EMPLOYEES

The first step towards introducing a no-smoking policy is to consult with the workforce to advise them of their employer's intentions and to find out their views. A good way of finding out employees' views is to ask them to complete a questionnaire. Typical questions may include:

- whether employees consider themselves as:
  - a non-smoker
  - an ex-smoker
  - a smoker who would like to give up
  - a smoker who does not intend to give up
  - whether tobacco smoke causes employees any problems eg:
  - headaches
  - sore throats
  - sore eyes
  - breathing difficulties
  - other problems

- whether employees would prefer to see smoking restricted to certain times of the day and/or banned in various areas of the organisation eg:

  - open plan offices

  - personal offices

  - staff restaurant

  - meeting rooms

  - lifts

  - corridors

  - toilets

  - interview rooms

- whether smokers would take advantage of help at work to give up or reduce their smoking if it were available

The answers can then be studied by the working party to gauge the depth of support for the various options which the working party may be considering. It is also a good idea to publish the results of the survey, whilst maintaining individuals' confidentiality, so that all employees are kept informed.

DRAFTING THE SMOKING POLICY

Depending upon the size of the working party, it may be better to set up a small sub-committee to prepare the draft policy rather than try to prepare the document with the full complement of members wishing to contribute! Once the draft has been prepared then it may be tested on the working party and once approved again tested on a sample of employees for their comments before adopting the final version.

The policy should clearly state:

- the principle that all employees have the right to breathe air that is free from tobacco smoke

- the date when the policy is to be implemented

- whether there is to be an initial period of time eg 3 months, when smoking will be restricted to specified times

- whether smoking is to be totally banned from all or certain work areas

- whether smoking facilities are to be made available and when they may be used

- who will be responsible for monitoring the implementation and enforcement of the policy

- what action will be taken against offenders to the policy

- what help is available to smokers wishing to give up

- whether the employer reserves the right to review or extend the policy at some future date at its discretion

IMPLEMENTING THE SMOKING POLICY

Once the final policy has been agreed all employees should be made aware of the arrangements and a date announced for implementation of the policy. Ideally, twelve weeks' notice should be given of the implementation date. A lesser period may be seen as an unreasonable period of time to enable employees to make the necessary adjustments.

The new smoking policy will need to be integrated into the terms and conditions of employment, including the Disciplinary Rules and Procedures, the Company Handbook, the Health and Safety Policy, recruitment and induction policies.

If a smoking area is to be provided then these facilities need to be prepared particularly bearing in mind suitable ventilation to cope with the smoky atmosphere.

No smoking signs will need to be posted and ash trays removed from no smoking areas.

Arrangements to help employees give up smoking will need to be set up.

UPHOLDING THE SMOKING POLICY

It is essential that the policy is enforced at all levels of the organisation regardless of seniority.

Normally, a failure to follow a no-smoking policy would be dealt with by offering guidance and counselling. However, if this failed to bring about the desired results then there might be no alternative but to follow the appropriate stages of the Disciplinary Procedure for a failure to observe the organisation's rules.

In certain areas of the workplace it may be that smoking may cause a very serious health and safety risk, for example where chemicals or other inflammable substances may be stored. Under such circumstances it may be that a smoking offence would be considered as gross misconduct which could lead to a summary dismissal.

Visitors to the organisation should be made aware of the smoking policy, for example by putting up notices in the Reception area or on entrances to the building.

REVIEW THE POLICY ON A REGULAR BASIS

It is a good idea to review the smoking policy on a regular basis, eg annually, to ensure that it is meeting the needs of the organisation as well as recognising the needs of its employees. For example smoking may be allowed on a restricted basis but there may be a wish to extend this to a full smoking ban at a later date.

ORGANISATIONS THAT PROVIDE HELP WITH SMOKING ISSUES

The following organisations will provide advice and guidance on issues related to smoking:

Action on Smoking and Health (ASH)
109 Gloucester Place
London
W1H 3PH

Telephone No. 071 935 3519

Health Education Authority
Hamilton House
Mabledon Place
London
WC1H 9TX

Telephone No. 071 631 0930

QUIT
102 Gloucester Place
London
W1H 3DA

Telephone No. 071 487 3000

PERSONAL APPEARANCE

WHAT IS ACCEPTABLE?

An issue which frequently causes a great deal of contention between employers and employees is reaching common agreement on what is acceptable dress and appearance in the workplace.

Views will vary dramatically depending upon the nature and size of the organisation as well as the culture. For example financial institutions which have a great deal of contact with the general public may require their employees to wear smart conventional dress whereas in a more creative environment such as an advertising studio or agency the accepted dress standards may well be more casual.

There are many jobs where the wearing of uniforms or special clothing is accepted as a requirement of the position.

There are a number of jobs where it is necessary to be able to distinguish employees from the general public, for example police officers, security guards, ticket inspectors and shop assistants, to enable them to carry out their duties.

In other jobs it may be necessary to provide a uniform as a form of protective clothing such as overalls, safety footwear or safety helmets to protect employees from the physical nature of the job or from a hygiene point of view in a kitchen where the wearing of hats, overalls or aprons may be a requirement.

DETERMINING STANDARDS OF APPEARANCE

An employer is entitled to set the standards of dress and appearance that it requires of its employees particularly where they will come into contact with members of the public.

CASE STUDY

For example, in Lumber v Hodder t/a Athletes Foot, COIT 1991, Mr Lumber was employed as an assistant in a sports shop where he was required to look smart and wear sports clothes so that he as well as the other members of staff portrayed a clean cut sporting image.

When Mr Lumber turned up wearing an earring, his boss, Mr Hodder, told him that he was not to wear the earring, or a sleeper, and Mr Lumber initially complied. Some time later Mr Lumber turned up at work wearing the earring again and following his refusal to remove it he was dismissed.

Mr Lumber claimed sex discrimination but was unsuccessful on the basis that Mr Hodder had not treated Mr Lumber any less favourably than he would have treated a woman if she had insisted on wearing clothes or accessories which did not fit in with the image he was trying to create in his sports shop.

Standards of appearance are not necessarily limited to dress and accessories. If an employer is trying to project a certain image as in the example stated above then the way hair is worn may be restricted by the employer. For example, in a conventional environment employees may be required to ensure that their hair is kept neat and tidy and the men may be prohibited from wearing their hair long.

Where food is being sold or prepared, in addition to hair being kept neat and tidy and under control, there may additionally be rules regarding beards.

CASE STUDY

In Singh v RHM Bakeries (Southern) Limited Mr Singh was dismissed for wearing a beard and long hair. He had previously complied with the company's rules which had been imposed in the interests of hygiene, but he had been re-affirmed in his faith and returned from a holiday dressed as an orthodox Sikh. The EAT supported the Tribunal's view that while the rule was discriminatory it could be justified on grounds of hygiene.

MAKING THE STANDARDS KNOWN

These standards should be recorded in the organisation's rules and procedures or in the Employee Handbook so that all employees are aware of the requirements.

As stated above, many employers require their employees to wear uniforms to distinguish them from members of the public or, it may be, to project a company image. Others may provide uniforms as protective clothing as well as to project their image, for example, catering staff, rescue staff (eg AA), factory and warehouse staff.

The rules should also be made known to prospective employees at interview so that they know what is expected and can decide beforehand whether they wish to accept employment under those circumstances.

LEGAL IMPLICATIONS

Care should be taken in determining required standards of dress and appearance so that the rules laid down do not unwittingly discriminate indirectly. For example, it could not be justified to refuse to allow a female Muslim to wear her traditional style trousers simply because all the women were required to wear overalls as a uniform in the style of a dress over their skirts.

To impose a condition or requirement that cannot be justified and with which a majority of either men or women, or people of a particular race, nationality or ethnic origin would be unable to comply may be indirect discrimination.

According to the EAT (1977), in Schmidt v Austicks Bookshops Limited, there is no discrimination on grounds of sex where there are comparable rules for both men and women restricting what may be worn at work and concerning appearance even though the rules may be different given the difference between the sexes.

CASE STUDY

In Burrett v West Birmingham Health Authority, Mrs Burrett was employed as a nurse in a hospital. Both men and women at the hospital were required to wear uniforms. The female nurses were required to wear hats and there were some units in the hospital, including the department in which she worked, where the requirement to wear hats did not apply to the men. Mrs Burrett took exception to this and was disciplined for refusing to wear her hat and

Case Study (continued)
transferred to a different department. Her claim of
sex discrimination was dismissed on the basis that
although the uniform was not the same for men and
women it did not amount to less favourable treatment
because of the differences in the uniform or because she
objected to a particular aspect of the uniform. There
was a policy that both men and women must wear a
prescribed uniform and there was nothing to suggest that
women could not comply with that requirement.

MAINTAINING STANDARDS

If an employer does expect a good standard of appearance
then it is important to ensure that any lapses in standards
are dealt with as they occur. If they are ignored then it
will be assumed that they are condoned.

As with other instances where company rules and
regulations have been disregarded, an attempt should be
made to correct lapses in standards of appearance in the
first instance by informal discussion and counselling.

If this fails to bring the offender back into line then the
complaint should be dealt with by following the normal
disciplinary procedures for conduct which could ultimately
lead to dismissal.

INTRODUCING CODES OF DRESS
AND APPEARANCE

If there is no standard established, then the introduction
of a standard should be discussed and agreed with
employees' representatives and made known to all

employees giving them reasonable advance warning of the organisation's requirements and the reasons why the employer wishes to introduce the changes.

If despite prior consultations and prior warning of the changes, an employee refuses to comply with the requirements, then it will be for the employer to apply the disciplinary code.

PERSONAL HYGIENE

DUCKING THE ISSUE

One of the problems which line or personnel managers dread having to deal with is with employees who suffer from unpleasant body odours or bad breath. Sadly, these matters tend to come to light following complaints from work colleagues who may already have tried to resolve the matter in their own way and failed.

Often, where there is a body odour or bad breath problem the individual becomes ostracised by the work group or may even be being bullied because he or she is regarded as socially unacceptable. Either way, this is likely to be to the detriment of the employee's effectiveness. If the employee is ostracised, while it may not affect him or her mentally, it may affect the way in which tasks are performed because of the lack of communication or contact that will result. If the employee is bullied then he or she may eventually suffer from stress and other anxiety disorders as a result of the bullying. This too is likely to affect both employee's attendance record and his or her work performance if allowed to continue.

Tackling the problem rather than ducking the issue could save the organisation a lot of time, money and unpleasantness.

IDENTIFYING THE CAUSE OF THE PROBLEM

There are a number of problems which could result in an employee suffering from body odours or bad breath. For example, it may be simply a matter of personal cleanliness and grooming; it could be the result of an individual's diet; it may be the side effect of a medical condition. It may be that the problem is not one that can be easily resolved.

DEALING WITH THE PROBLEM

If there is an occupational health department within the organisation, it would probably be more acceptable for the employee to be steered towards the company nurse for an informal chat.

If there is no occupational health department then the problem usually falls into the lap of the Personnel Department or Line Manager. Where this is the case it would be less embarrassing for the person to be approached by a person more senior to him or her and of the same sex.

The discussions should be kept confidential and the employee should be counselled to

- try to find out if he or she is aware of the problem

- offer help and guidance in tackling the problem.

BODY ODOURS

There are a number of body odours which are linked to the way we live and what we eat and a degree of tolerance should be shown to people from different cultures or different lifestyles.

For example a North European who uses only limited seasonings such as salt and pepper in his or her food, drinks beer and smokes cigarettes will have different body odours from a South European who eats food laced with garlic and other herbs and drinks mainly wine. An Asian who eats mainly food flavoured with curry spices and drinks mainly tea will be different again.

Someone who jogs or rides a bicycle to work will emit different odours from someone who travels by train or by car. A smoker or someone who travels in a car with a smoker or in a smoking compartment of a train will smell differently again.

PERSONAL HYGIENE

Instances do occur where employees do not wash sufficiently often or thoroughly or do not change their clothes regularly.

Often with personal hygiene problems the person concerned may be unaware that he or she is causing offence to others. The person who has to speak to the employee may well be more embarrassed than the person to whom he or she has to convey such a message.

The simplest way to tackle the issue may be to approach the problem head on by opening discussions by saying something like 'I know that this may embarrass us both but there are matters which we simply have to discuss. I have received a number of complaints from people who are bothered by your body odours. Can you try and do something about it.' Once the topic has been broached it will become easier to talk constructively and supportively, and hopefully that in itself will be sufficient to get the message across and resolve the matter.

CASE STUDY

George was training to be an accountant with a small firm of Chartered Accountants. He had until recently lived at home with his parents where his mother had ruled the roost, telling both him and his

---

Case Study (continued)

younger brother when they were permitted to take baths, wash their hair and change their clothes.

George later moved into his own flat and became responsible for organising his own personal hygiene and washing with the result that he did not change his clothes sufficiently frequently or bath regularly. After a number of complaints had been made by George's colleagues to the senior partner in the firm, the senior partner's secretary, who was well liked and a more mature person whom the younger people in the partnership respected, volunteered to speak to George.

This approach worked well under the circumstances. George, who was a shy and retiring young man, did not feel embarrassed by being spoken to by the senior secretary and gratefully accepted her suggestions on how to establish a better routine now that he no longer lived at home with his parents. He was grateful that the matter had been brought to his attention before it created difficulties in his working relationships with his colleagues.

If the problem is not resolved through counselling then it should be suggested that the employee seeks advice from his or her own medical adviser.

If it appears that informal discussions will not resolve the matter and the person concerned is unwilling to take steps to solve the problem then it may be necessary to go through the disciplinary process which could ultimately lead to dismissal.

A MEDICAL PROBLEM

If the problem is not one that the employee can resolve through personal hygiene then consideration should be given to allowing the person time off to seek advice from his or her own medical practitioner or the organisation's medical adviser. If resources permit, referral to a private medical clinic would be ideal.

If the employee is willing, it would improve employee relations if the individual's immediate colleagues were advised of the problem in confidence so that the attitudes of workmates are more likely to be supportive if they know that there is a medical problem rather than destructive because they believe that the individual affected is simply not washing regularly!

It may be possible to look at subtle ways of re-organising the working environment so that the effect on the employee's colleagues is minimised without causing embarrassment to the person concerned.

DISHONESTY

An employer may be faced with a problem of dishonesty in the workplace itself or it may involve the criminal conduct of an employee outside of work.

Examples of dishonesty may include:

- Theft of money or property

- Fraud

- Falsification of records eg timesheets, expense claims.

DISHONESTY IN THE WORKPLACE

Industrial Tribunals will consider dismissal for conduct as one of the potentially fair reasons for dismissal. However, an employer must first prove the grounds for the dismissal and then show that it was fair to dismiss for that reason. In other words, the employer must show that it was reasonable to dismiss under the circumstances and that any reasonable employer might have dismissed under similar circumstances bearing in mind that in all cases there is a band of reasonableness within which one employer might reasonably take a different view from another.

Normally acts of dishonesty in the workplace will be regarded as sufficiently serious by the courts to warrant summary dismissal, ie, dismissal without a further warning, and most employers will include dishonesty as one of the offences which are classified as gross misconduct in their Disciplinary Rules and Procedures.

The ACAS Code of Practice on Disciplinary Procedures requires employers to spell out the Disciplinary Rules and Procedures applicable to them and this includes giving examples of the offences which could lead to dismissal. These rules should be issued or made readily available to employees and a verbal explanation given, for example as part of the induction programme, so that they are fully understood.

By including dishonesty as an example of gross misconduct in the Disciplinary Rules the employer is in effect giving employees prior warning that such offences would lead to dismissal without further disciplinary warnings being given. However, even if theft is omitted from a list of examples of gross misconduct, it will not preclude the employer from summarily dismissing for theft.

To ensure that the dismissal is seen to be fair, ACAS has laid down a checklist of the steps which employers should follow to ensure that the principles of natural justice are applied. They are:

GATHER ALL THE FACTS BEFORE MEMORIES FADE

All the facts that are available should be gathered including taking statements and collecting documents where appropriate as soon as possible before memories fade to ensure that a thorough investigation is carried out.

INFORM THE EMPLOYEE OF THE ALLEGATIONS

The employee should be notified in writing of the allegations which are being made against him or her so that he or she has the opportunity of preparing his or her side of the case in advance of the hearing, giving ample opportunity to gather the facts, take statements from colleagues, and generally prepare himself or herself before the disciplinary hearing so that he or she is able to put forward any mitigating circumstances which he or she wishes to be taken into consideration.

INFORM THE EMPLOYEE THAT THE INTERVIEW IS OF A DISCIPLINARY NATURE

The employee should be advised in writing that the hearing is to be of a disciplinary nature so that he or she is aware of the seriousness of the matter.

INFORM THE EMPLOYEE THAT HE OR SHE IS ENTITLED TO HAVE HIS OR HER REPRESENTATIVE PRESENT AT THE HEARING

When the employee is informed that the hearing is to be of a disciplinary nature he or she should be reminded, in writing, that he or she is entitled to have his or her representative present.

INTERVIEW THE EMPLOYEE MAKING SURE THAT HE OR SHE HAS EVERY OPPORTUNITY TO PUT HIS OR HER SIDE OF THE CASE

At the interview the employee should be reminded of the purpose of the hearing and where appropriate evidence to support the allegations should be presented to him or her. This may include showing papers or other documentation and it may be that witnesses will be required to make statements on behalf of the employer.

The employee should be given every opportunity to respond to the allegations and to put forward his or her own papers, documentation or invite witnesses to give statements in support of his or her case so that any mitigating circumstances can be fully considered.

PAUSE

After the employer has explained the allegations to the employee and the employee in turn has put his or her side of the case, it is important that the meeting is adjourned so that full consideration can be given to the facts of the case and all the options considered before any disciplinary decision is taken.

If new information has come to light then it may be necessary to undertake further investigations so that this can be properly considered before a decision is made.

RIGHT OF APPEAL

The employee should be made aware that he or she has the right to appeal against any decision which is taken. He or she should be advised who he or she should appeal to and the time limit in which to do so.

This appeal should be conducted by someone who has not been connected with the disciplinary decision and at a more senior level than the person who took the decision to dismiss.

In a small organisation it may be more appropriate for the appeal to be heard either by another senior person not connected with the matter or it may be agreed between the parties that an independent person, acceptable to both sides, be brought in to hear the appeal.

If it is decided that the same person will have to hear the appeal because of the size and resources of the organisation, then it is important to leave a few days' gap between the dismissal decision and the appeal hearing, to allow emotions to cool and so enable the person hearing the appeal to act as objectively as possible.

In cases of theft it is not always possible to prove beyond reasonable doubt that an employee has committed the offence even though a full and proper investigation may indicate that the employee did in fact commit the offence.

CASE STUDY

In British Home Stores Limited v Burchell (EAT 1978) Miss Burchell was dismissed for allegedly being involved with a number of other employees concerning staff purchases. Miss Burchell had charged a colleague for a pair of expensive sunglasses at the price of a less expensive pair even though, in the opinion of management, she knew the correct price to be charged.

EAT laid down the following guidelines in determining whether dismissal will be seen to be reasonable:

- 'There must be established by the employer the fact of that belief, that the employer did believe it

- It must be shown that the employer had in his mind reasonable grounds upon which to sustain that belief

- The employer at the stage in which he formed that belief on those grounds must have carried out as much investigation into the matter as was reasonable in all the circumstances of the case.'

In other words, the employer must be able to show that he was convinced that the employee had committed the act of dishonesty, even though he may not be able to prove it, having carried out a thorough investigation into the matter.

There may be circumstances whereby an employer suspects one or more employees to be guilty of misconduct but is unable to identify a single employee as the culprit. In this situation the employer may be justified in dismissing all the employees involved.

CASE STUDY

In Monie v Coral Racing Limited (CA 1980), Mr Monie was employed as an Area Manager in charge of 19 betting shops. Only he and his assistant knew the combination of the safe at area headquarters. Mr Monie had called into the office prior to going off on holiday. Several days later his assistant went to the safe and discovered that £1750 was missing. There was no indication of a break in either to the safe or the premises. Both Mr Monie and his assistant were interviewed and the conclusion was drawn that one or both of them must have been involved in the theft. They were both subsequently dismissed on the basis that 'since there was no indication at the inquiry which of you was responsible for the cash deficit I have no alternative but to instantly dismiss both of you.'

The Court of Appeal upheld the view that where an employer reasonably believes that theft is the work of one of two employees or possibly both but cannot distinguish between them he can act reasonably if he dismisses both.

CASE STUDY

These principles were applied in the case of Whitbread & Co Plc t/a Ashe & Nephews v Thomas and others. In this case the three respondents were employed as part-time assistants in the off-licence. There had been a problem with stock losses over a number of years and the employers had been unable to identify the cause of the stock losses despite extensive efforts. The employees concerned were given warnings and were also transferred to other shops for a short period. During this time there were no problems with stock losses either in their temporary shop or their normal place of work. Following their return matters became worse than ever and they were eventually dismissed for failing to prevent the stock losses.

The following guidelines were laid down when dealing with blanket dismissals such as this:

- An act (whether of commission or omission) has been committed which if committed by an identified individual would justify his or her dismissal.

- The Tribunal are satisfied that the act or acts were committed by one or more of a group, all of whom can be shown to be individually capable of having committed the act complained of. In this context commission includes omission.

- The Tribunal are satisfied that there has been a proper investigation by the employer to identify the person or persons responsible for the act (or commission or omission).

●If all three matters are satisfied then an employer who cannot identify which individual was responsible is entitled to dismiss all members of such a group even where it is possible or indeed probable that all were not guilty of the offence.

CRIMINAL PROCEEDINGS

It is up to the employers to carry out a full and proper investigation following which they are entitled to make a decision based on the information available to them at the time.

There is no need to wait for the outcome of police enquiries or court proceedings before making a decision. The key requirement is that the employee is given the opportunity to put forward his or her own representations in mitigation of the compliant prior to a decision being reached.

CRIMINAL OFFENCES OUTSIDE WORK

Criminal offences committed outside work should not automatically be treated as reasons for dismissal.

Consideration should be given as to whether the offence is one which is likely to make it unsuitable for the employee to continue to carry out his or her type of work or whether it makes him or her unacceptable to other employees. An employee should not be dismissed simply because there is a criminal charge pending against him or her, or because he or she has been remanded in custody.

The following matters should be taken into account when considering whether criminal offences outside work should affect whether or not the employee's employment should continue or whether he or she should be dismissed:

- The nature of the offence

- The status of the employee and the nature of the job

- The impact on the employer/employee relationship

- The extent to which the relationship is capable of any further performance.

For example on Lloyds Bank plc v Bardin (EAT 1989), Ms Bardin was employed as a part-time cleaner. She was dismissed after admitting that she had obtained money by deception. The EAT decided that the issue was not whether Ms Bardin was a security risk but whether Lloyds had acted reasonably in all the circumstances. The dismissal was upheld on the basis that there was an adequate link between the offence and the nature of Ms Bardin's work to justify the employer's actions.

It is unlikely that a similar view would have been taken had Ms Bardin been employed as a cleaner in an environment where the employer's business was of a totally different nature eg food processing or car manufacture.

IMPRISONMENT

Imprisonment in itself is not sufficient grounds on which to dismiss an employee.

Leaving aside the reasons for the imprisonment, such factors as the likely duration of the imprisonment, whether or not an appeal has any chance of success, the nature of the employee's work and status within the organisation will all have an impact on whether or not it is fair to dismiss.

DISMISSAL FOR PREVIOUS CONVICTIONS

Under the Rehabilitation of Offenders Act 1974, employees or prospective employees are not required to disclose convictions which are regarded as 'spent'. A conviction is regarded as 'spent', in other words it should be disregarded, if the offender has completed both the sentence and the rehabilitation period with good behaviour.

If a conviction is 'spent', the offender is entitled to withhold information concerning the offence to a prospective employer.

It also means that a prospective employer may not ask an applicant if he or she has a 'spent' conviction although he may ask if he or she has convictions. If the convictions are spent then an applicant may answer 'no'. In other words a spent conviction may be treated as though it had never occurred.

If an employer dismisses an employee after he finds out that an employee has a 'spent' conviction then it will be an unfair dismissal.

If an employer discovers that an employee has not disclosed a conviction that is not 'spent' then dismissal may be fair depending upon the nature of the employment and the employer's reasons for the termination.

SUSPENDED SENTENCES

All suspended sentences are treated in the same way as sentences which have been served as far as rehabilitation periods are concerned. This means that if both the period of suspended sentence and the period of rehabilitation have been served, the conviction is regarded as 'spent' and should be treated in the same way as a sentence that was served.

EXAMPLES OF SENTENCES

Sentence	Rehabilitation Period	
	Age 17 or over on conviction	Age under 17 on conviction
Prison or young offender institution more than 6 months but less than 2 1/2 years	10 years	5 years
Prison or young offender institution 6 months or less	7 years	3 years
Fine or community service order	5 years	2 1/2 years
Absolute discharge	6 months	6 months
Probation, supervision, care order, conditional discharge or bind over	1 year or until order expires	Same
Attendance care order	1 year after order expirers	Same
Hospital order	5 years or 2 years after order expires	Same

EXCEPTIONS

The Act does not apply to any sentence of more than 2 1/2 years' duration.

The majority of professions are exempt from this Act, for example:

- Medical practitioners
- Nurses
- Midwives
- Veterinary surgeons
- Accountants
- Solicitors
- Barristers
- Opticians
- Teachers
- Pharmaceutical chemists
- Certain judicial and law enforcement officers
- Security Officers

In addition, those concerned with providing young people with care, leisure and recreational facilities, schooling, social services, supervision or training, and those providing the elderly, sick or disabled people with health or social services, are exempt.

TACKLING DISHONESTY IN THE WORKPLACE

IDENTIFYING UNKNOWN SUSPECTS

Often it is difficult to identify who is actually the culprit when tackling problems of petty theft in the workplace.

If it is possible to identify a group of people who are affected by the problem, it may be worth holding a meeting to advise them of the problem and to seek their help as an alternative to bringing in the police. They can be asked to volunteer information, in confidence, if they are able to shed any light on the matter in the hope that the issue may be resolved in house.

This may also be a way of encouraging the person who has actually committed the theft to come forward with the promise that any mitigating circumstances will be considered when deciding what, if any, action should be taken against him or her.

Depending upon what is being stolen and from where, it may be possible to arrange for surveillance to be undertaken with a view to catching the thief in the act. For example, it may be possible to introduce video cameras in such a way as to be able to alert those undertaking the surveillance and/or identify the culprit.

With the assistance of the police, goods or banknotes may be marked in such a way as to leave an indelible but invisible mark on the thief which can only be seen when it is exposed to certain lighting. If the goods or banknotes are removed then the police may be called to question the suspect.

SEARCHES OF EMPLOYEES AND THEIR PROPERTY

Many companies include in their terms and conditions of employment their right to be able to search an employee or his or her personal property such as a car or handbag whilst on company premises. Employees cannot be forced to undergo a search and if this is imposed upon them they could prosecute the employer on the basis of criminal assault.

Whether or not a clause is contained in the contract of employment, the employee may still be asked if he or she is willing to submit to a search.

If an employee withholds his or her agreement to be searched then the employer may choose to call in the police to carry out the search and/or take action through the disciplinary procedure if refusal would be in breach of contract.

PREVENTATIVE STRATEGIES

A number of retail organisations including Harrods and Dixons have introduced pro-active measures which include:

- Establishing clear policies on theft which include taking swift and decisive action when dealing with such matters either by employees or customers

- Raising staff awareness through induction training and re-inforcing the organisation's principles and actions by advertising what will happen to those that get caught

- Continually reviewing and revising procedures to reduce the opportunity for theft

DISABILITY AND MENTAL ILLNESS

THE DISABLED PERSONS (EMPLOYMENT) ACTS 1944 AND 1958

Under the Acts, employers with 20 or more employees are required to employ at least 3% registered disabled people. It is an offence for employers with below this percentage of registered disabled people in their employment to offer a job to a person who is not registered unless a permit allowing them to do so has been obtained from the Department of Employment.

The Acts provide that it is a criminal offence to dismiss a registered disabled person without reasonable cause if at the time the employer was below the quota of 3% or if the dismissal resulted in bringing the company below the quota.

Orders may be made under the Acts for certain employments to be designated as specially suitable for disabled persons. Currently the employments of passenger lift attendant and car park attendant are the only occupations to have been so designated.

Disability under the Acts includes disablement as a result of injury, disease or deformity.

CODE OF PRACTICE ON THE EMPLOYMENT OF DISABLED PEOPLE

There is a Code of Practice on the Employment of Disabled People produced by the Employment Service (available free of charge) which sets out the schemes that are available to help disabled people, including grants and provision of equipment to help the disabled in the workplace.

THE ADVANTAGES OF EMPLOYING PEOPLE WITH DISABILITIES AND MENTAL ILLNESS

Often, people with disabilities will work to a higher standard of work performance or have a better attendance record than able-bodied people.

The fact that an employer has been prepared to offer an opportunity for them to show that they can work just as well as other people will frequently result in a high degree of personal motivation and enthusiasm in tackling their work.

DIFFICULTIES THAT EMPLOYERS MAY FACE WHEN EMPLOYING PEOPLE WITH DISABILITIES AND MENTAL ILLNESS

Unfortunately people with disabilities or mental illness can cause problems for employers in a variety of different ways, for example:

- Prolonged or frequent periods of absence either resulting from disability or mental illness will make it difficult for the employer to plan and organise the work effectively.

- A person with disabilities or mental illness may find it increasingly difficult to carry out his or her duties to a standard which the employer finds acceptable.

- Mental illness can cause erratic or peculiar behaviour in the workplace which may be unacceptable or mean that the person is unable to carry out his or her work satisfactorily.

- Occasionally employers may face a situation where their employees may refuse to co-operate or have difficulty in accepting an employee with disabilities.

More often than not the situation can be resolved by counselling the employees so that they gain a greater understanding of the problems experienced by the disabled person and are therefore able to follow their employer's lead in being more sympathetic, understanding and supportive of their disabled colleague's situation.

In the event that an employee continues to fail to co-operate or work with a disabled person despite the employer's efforts to resolve the matter, then, depending upon the circumstances, it may be necessary to consider taking disciplinary action against that employee.

DISMISSALS

Dismissals connected with disability or mental illness must follow the general rules for dismissal and will be potentially fair provided that the employer has acted in a fair and reasonable way, bearing in mind the nature of the disability or illness, and providing that the correct procedures have been followed.

However, dismissals connected with mental illness should be handled with an even greater degree of caution than other health problems: Lord McDonald stated in Thompson v Strathclyde Regional Council (EAT 1983) that 'incapacity on the grounds of mental health is an exceptionally delicate and sensitive field'.

The following guidelines may be helpful when considering whether dismissal is appropriate, taking into account all the circumstances, eg the nature of the individual's health and his or her own personal limitations as well as the work which is available for him or her to do:

ABSENCES DUE TO INCAPACITY

As stated above, prolonged or frequent periods of absence can make it extremely difficult for an employer to manage the business effectively. How long an employer can continue to put up with this will depend on the size of organisation, the resources available and the nature of the work. Eventually, however, the employer may consider that enough is enough and that the situation cannot be allowed to continue.

As with all dismissials relating to health, a medical report should be sought from the employee's general practitioner to ensure that a thorough medical investigation has been undertaken. This will enable the employer to find out if and when the employee is likely to be fit enough to return to work either to his or her usual duties or to duties which are more suited to his or her medical condition.

Under the Access to Medical Reports Act 1988, an employee must give his or her written consent to enable the employer to obtain a medical report from his or her general practitioner. If an employee withholds his or her consent then he or she should be advised that a decision may have to be taken in the absence of information that could have an effect on his or her future employment with the organisation.

When seeking a medical report, it is important to provide the medical adviser with a brief description of the duties which the employee is normally required to undertake. This should include any physical aspects of the job such as driving, lifting, standing or walking, and the levels of concentration or decision making that are needed, so that a response can be given in the context of the employee's medical condition. It may be worth asking for advice on the sort of work that might be more appropriate for the employee so that investigations can be made to see if anything more suitable can be found if necessary.

In addition, the employee must be consulted with a view to discussing whether alternatives may be feasible in order to help him or her get back to work. For example, a change in some of the duties or re-arranged working hours may help the employee to get back to work. The possibility of providing new equipment which is more suited to the disabled person's abilities or adapting existing equipment should be investigated.

An employer is not obliged to create a position to suit the individual although a genuine attempt should be made to accommodate the employee particularly if this would enable him or her to return to work within the reasonably foreseeable future.

PERFORMANCE

Disability or mental illness may make it difficult for the employee to continue to perform his or her duties to a standard acceptable to the employer. This may occur suddenly as a result of an injury or illness occurring out of the blue, or performance may deteriorate over a period of time as a result of an existing condition deteriorating.

Even if an employer has put up with an employee's limitations for a long time but finds that circumstances make this difficult to allow it to continue, dismissal will be fair provided that proper warnings are given and a reasonable period of time is allowed for the individual to achieve the improvements in performance that are necessary.

As with incapacity absences described above, a full investigation should be carried out to determine the medical facts and whether or not the situation may improve and the timescales in which any improvements are envisaged. Sufficient time should be given to allow the employee to achieve an acceptable standard. If necessary, as with ordinary dismissals for performance, further training or coaching should first be considered to help the employee reach the standards required.

As above, the employee should be consulted and where appropriate alternatives considered. It is important that assumptions are not made concerning 'what the employer considers is best for the individual'. Without proper investigation and consultation with the employee, the wrong conclusions could be drawn about his or her capabilities. It could also show total disregard for the individual's own wishes.

BEHAVIOURAL PROBLEMS

In some cases, people with mental illness may become violent or behave in such a way that they may cause a serious safety hazard or serious disruption to the employer's business.

As before, a thorough investigation and consultation with the employee should be undertaken and the reasonableness of the decision to dismiss will depend upon the facts.

For example in Wright v Commissioners of Inland Revenue (EAT 1979) it was known when Mr Wright was appointed that he was a schizophrenic. After two years he started suffering delusions and was convinced that he was under surveillance by MI5, claiming that his doctor was in league with them. His behaviour caused severe disruptions in the office and eventually after medical investigations and lengthy meetings he was fairly dismissed on the grounds of incapability.

CONDUCT

Occasionally individuals with mental illness may behave in such a way that they have seriously breached codes of conduct. Under these circumstances allowance must be made taking into account the medical condition of the employee in determining what action should be taken against him or her.

As before, a thorough investigation and consultation with the employee should be undertaken and the reasonableness of the decision to dismiss will depend upon the facts.

CASE STUDY

In Peacock v Vi-Seal Tapes Limited (COIT) the company were aware that Mr Peacock suffered from depression and was known to drink. He had already been given a disciplinary warning for absenteeism and lateness and was subsequently dismissed for failing to send in a medical certificate following a week's absence. The dismissal was found to be unfair as the company

> **Case Study** (continued)
> had been notified that he was suffering from another spell of depression and they had not carried out a proper investigation. However, Mr Peacock's compensation was reduced by 75% for contributory conduct.

DIRECTORS' REPORTS

Under the Companies (Directors' Report) (Employment of Disabled Persons) Regulations 1980, a statement must be included in the Annual Report of a company which employs more than an average number of 250 employees in the financial year.

This statement must set out the policy that the company has applied that year in relation to disabled persons:

- for giving full and fair consideration to applications for employment by disabled persons taking into account their particular aptitudes and abilities

- for enabling those who have become disabled to continue in employment by arranging for appropriate training

- for offering training, career development and promotion opportunities for disabled persons employed by the company.